Tales and Legends from India

RUSKIN BOND

Illustrated by Sally Scott

JM

Julia MacRae Books

A DIVISION OF FRANKLIN WATTS

First published in Great Britain by
Julia MacRae Books
A division of Franklin Watts Ltd
8 Cork Street, London, W1X 2HA
and Franklin Watts Inc.
730 Fifth Avenue, New York 10019

Typeset by Computape (Pickering) Ltd, North Yorkshire
Printed in Great Britain by Camelot Press, Southampton

Also by Ruskin Bond
THE ROAD TO THE BAZAAR
FLAMES IN THE FOREST (Blackbird Series)

British Library Cataloguing in Publication Data

Tales and legends from India.
1. Tales, India – Juvenile literature
2. Legends, India – Juvenile literature
I. Bond, Ruskin   II. Scott, Sally
398.2'0954   GR305

ISBN 0-86203-044-7 UK edition
ISBN 0-531-04073-9 US edition
Library of Congress Catalog Card No:
80-85296

For Rakesh, Mukesh and Savitri

Contents

Introduction

SHEHERAZADE, whose life depended upon her ability to turn out one tale after another, night after Arabian night, would, I am sure, have approved of my devoting most of my life to story-telling. Although in no danger of being executed for failing to meet a deadline (could that be how the word came into being?), my life has in many ways depended upon my story-telling abilities, which have been the best and only way in which I have been able to make a living – and also choose the place of my abode, the foothills of the Himalayas.

For over twenty-five years, ever since I was a boy out of school in Simla, I have been a professional teller of tales – short stories, tall stories, folk-stories, true stories, unfinished stories.... I am still a long way from Sheherazade's thousand and one tales, but then, I haven't had the executioner's axe poised over me, spurring me on: only the rent to pay and books to buy and an occasional chicken for my supper, prepared by Prem Singh, who cooks chickens better than I write stories. Prem and his family live with me, and it is his children, and their demands for stories, that keep me inventing new tales or digging up old ones such as those in this collection.

My early stories, written when I was in my twenties, were about my own childhood in India and some of the people I knew as I grew up. Then, in my thirties, I wrote about other Indian children – some of them are in *The Road to the Bazaar*, also published by Julia MacRae. Now in my forties, I find myself going even further back in time, to the young heroes and heroines, Gods and Demons, of myth, legend and folklore. Although my father was British, I grew up an Indian, and have always cherished the literature of both East and West. There has been no division of loyalties; only a double inheritance.

Some of the responsibility for my interest in folklore must lie (literally) at the door of the mother of my friend Anil Singh, whose ancestral home is in a village not far from Agra. Long before I came to "dwell in the Himalayan country" (to use a phrase from *The Jataka*), I spent a winter in my friend's village in the plains, where I soon discovered that his mother had at her command a great store of folklore, and there was nothing she liked better than to tell me stories in the evening gloam — at "cow-dust time", that brief Indian twilight — before she went indoors to prepare our dinner. She would recline on a string cot in the courtyard, puffing at a hookah, recounting old tales of ghosts, fairies and other familiars. Two or three of these tales appear in this collection. There were more; but room had to be made for a wider selection — tales representative of different parts of the country, of followers of different faiths, of tribal peoples, kings and commoners. I have leant heavily on the great Hindu religious epic, *The Mahabharata*, in which so many enchanting stories are found; on the Buddhist fables in *The Jataka*; and on the early renderings of pioneering folklorists, Indian and British. In a section of Notes, which I have compiled with as much care as I have retold the stories, I have given the sources and the background to the tales and legends.

I am fortunate to be living and working in the mountains, in full view of the majestic snow-peaks of the furthest Himalayan ranges — those same peaks where the gods and goddesses of Hindu mythology have their abode. And I am doubly fortunate in being able to look down from the mountains upon the plains of India, a melting-pot of races and religions, where so much has happened, and still happens, to excite the mind and spirit. India is more than a land – it is an atmosphere – and this book is designed to give the reader the feel of India and recapture some of its old magic.

Ruskin Bond
Mussoorie, India

Tales from the Epics

Love Conquers All

LONG LONG AGO there was a king who ruled over a large part of India. He was a great horseman, and when he rode he was like a strong wind rushing by. Horses knew and loved him, and because of his power over them he was known as the Lord-of-Horses.

In spite of his fame and popularity, the king was unhappy, for no children had been born to him, and in India this was always considered a great calamity. He went from temple to temple, praying and offering sacrifices, but to no avail – it seemed as though the gods were displeased with him.

Finally he consulted the great sage Narada.

"How can I please the gods?" he asked. "I have been married five years, but still there is no heir to the throne."

"Build a new temple," said Narada. "Build a temple to Brahma the Creator."

"I shall build the most beautiful temple in the land," said the king, and he immediately summoned his best workmen and told them to build a temple taller than any other.

"Let it be taller than three palm trees," he said. "Paint it gold within and gold without. A hundred steps of pure white marble must lead up to it."

Within a few months a beautiful golden temple was built, surrounded by flowering trees and shrubs. And every day the king visited the temple, making special offerings to Brahma, God of Creation, and his wife, Savitri, that they might send him a son.

His queen and his nobles, and even the sage Narada, had almost given up hope, when one day, as the king laid his offerings before the shrine, he thought he saw a figure growing out of the flames that had sprung up from his sacrifice. And then he heard a voice – the voice, he thought, of a goddess, because though it was small and sweet it filled the temple with its sound.

"You have pleased me with your devotion," were the words he heard. "I am Savitri, wife of Brahma. What is it you seek?"

His voice trembling, the king said, "Goddess, I desire a son, so that my name may not perish from the land."

"I will give you a daughter," replied the clear sweet voice.

The fire died down and the figure faded.

And not long afterwards there was great rejoicing in the king's palace. A daughter was born to the queen – a girl so radiantly beautiful that her parents were convinced that she was heaven-born, and sent out a proclamation saying that the child was to be called "Savitri" after the wife of Brahma.

As Savitri grew up, her father began to think about her marriage, and he decided that she should choose a husband for herself from among the princes of the neighbouring states. He had no intention of imposing his will upon her.

"Daughter," he said one day, "do you wish to marry? You may, if you wish, visit the palaces of our neighbouring kings and choose a husband for yourself from among the princes. I know that you are as wise as you are lovely, and that your choice will be pleasing to me."

Savitri decided that she would seek her husband, not among her wealthy and royal neighbours, but among the remote dwellings of the hermits in the forest. She had her chariot prepared for a long journey, and ordered her drivers to take the path that led into the wilderness.

After driving through the forest for several hours, the chariot-drivers told Savitri that a hermitage lay ahead. Savitri and her handmaidens got down from the chariot and approached a small temple, beside which stood a hut made of leaves and branches. Inside the hut they found an old man who, though blind and white-haired, had an upright bearing. He was, in fact, not a priest, but a king: many years ago he had gone blind and had been driven from his kingdom by a rival who took over his throne and threatened death to any of the king's family who tried to return.

As Savitri stood watching the blind old man, a youth on a black horse came riding through the forest and up to the door of the hut.

"He dresses like a peasant," said Savitri to herself, "but he sits his horse like a prince." And when she saw his face, her own lit up, for she knew that she had seen the man she would marry.

The youth dismounted, tethered his horse, greeted the old man with tender affection, and went into the hut.

"We need search no further," said Savitri to her handmaidens. "Let us ask the hospitality of these good people, and then in a few days we will return home."

The old king made them welcome. He told them of his misfortunes and of how he, and his wife, and their little son Satyavan, had been driven from the kingdom of Shalwa twenty years ago, and had lived ever since among the hermits of the forest. Satyavan stood aside, watching Savitri, and falling further in love with her every moment. Not many days had passed before they had vowed to marry each other, but Savitri said that first she must return to her father's kingdom and obtain his consent to the marriage, after which she would come back to the forest and follow Satyavan for the rest of her life.

"But do not tell your parents as yet," she said. "Let me first speak to my father."

Savitri returned to her father's palace and found him holding counsel with Narada. The sage had suggested that it was time that a husband was found for Savitri.

"Well, here she is," said the king, as Savitri approached. "She will tell you whether or not she has found a husband."

"Yes, father, I have," she cried, as she knelt at his feet for blessing. "In his dress and his possessions he is a poor man's son, but by birth he is a prince."

"And his name?"

"Satyavan."

Before she could say another word, Narada, looking horrified, stood up and with raised hand, said: "No, Princess, not Satyavan!"

"There can be no other," said Savitri with a smile.

The king turned to Narada and asked: "Is there something wrong with the youth? Is he not all that my daughter takes him for?"

"He is all that she says ... "

"Then is he already betrothed? Is there a curse upon him?"

Narada bowed his head and in a low voice said: "He is destined for an early death. Yama, the God of Death, has set his noose for him. Within a year the prince must die."

Savitri went pale, and almost fainted. But she summoned up all her courage and said, "Narada, you have prophesied his doom. I can but pray and hope. But even the knowledge of this terrible fate cannot shake my purpose. Satyavan shall be my husband for a year, even if for fifty I must be a widow!"

The sage stood silent, his head sunk upon his breast. Then finally he raised his hands towards Savitri in blessing.

"Peace be with you, daughter of the Lord-of-Horses," he said, and turned and walked away.

The next day it was announced that the Princess Savitri would soon marry a prince in a distant region, and that, since the journey would be long and tedious, only her father would accompany her. Preparations were soon made, and the Lord-of-Horses and his beautiful daughter set out for the forest. They took with them many costly gifts for the parents of the bridegroom. But when the old King of the Shalwas heard what had brought them to his home, he was taken aback.

"But how can this be?" he asked. "How will your heaven-sent daughter fare in this rough country? There are no maids to tend on her. And what shall we feed her? We eat the fruits of the forest. We sleep on an earthen floor."

Savitri took the blind old man by the hand, and spoke to him so sweetly and gently that she removed all his fears.

That same evening, when Satyavan returned from hunting, Savitri was given to him in marriage. The only guests were the hermits who lived near by. All they brought as gifts were their blessings; and Savitri pleased them by removing her jewels and replacing her rich garments with humble clothes.

The Lord-of-Horses bade his daughter farewell, and rode alone back to his kingdom.

The days and weeks and months slipped by, and it seemed to Satyavan that his wife grew lovelier and more gentle by the hour. No man was as happy as he. Savitri, too, was happy; but as the day of doom approached, she became quiet and pensive. She decided she would not leave his side by day or night. So she watched and waited, and seldom slept.

One morning the blind old king asked Satyavan to go to a part of the forest where there was a bamboo grove. He asked him to cut and bring home several stout pieces of bamboo.

When Satyavan set out, Savitri decided to follow him.

Satyavan, whistling cheerfully, soon reached the place where the bamboos grew, and raised his axe; but he had scarcely lifted it above his head for the first stroke, when it fell from his hands. He sank to the ground.

Savitri, following close behind, knew that the fatal moment was at hand. She ran forward and took his head in her arms. A shadow fell over them, and she became aware of a terrible form bending over her. He was tall and gaunt, greenish in hue, but with eyes of a fiery red. He carried a noose in one of his hands.

This was Yama, the God of Death.

Savitri rose slowly from the ground and, bending low before Yama, said: "What do you want, oh mighty one?"

"I have come for Satyavan, whose term of life is ended." And Yama leant forward and drew the prince's soul right out of his body.

Then, turning to the south, he fled at lightning speed.

But Savitri, too, was fleet of foot. Love lent her wings, and she followed close at Yama's heels. They came at last to the edge of the world, beyond which no mortal may pass alive, and here the God of Death stopped and spoke.

"Return, Savitri! You have followed far enough. Return and bury your husband's body with due rites."

"No, great Yama," answered Savitri. "When I wed my lord, I vowed to follow him, wherever he went or was taken. I have done no wrong since I made that vow, and so the gods have no power over me to make me break it."

"That is true," said Yama," and your answer pleases me. Ask a boon of me — but not the gift of your husband's life!"

Savitri thought for a moment, and then asked that the old King of the Shalwas should regain his sight.

"It is granted," said Yama. "Now return. No mortal may pass this spot alive."

But Savitri stood her ground. She knew that no one loved Yama, that he was friendless even among the gods, so she decided to flatter him.

"Is it true, oh Yama, that a mortal is pleasing to the gods if she mingles with those who are virtuous?"

"It is true," said Yama.

"Then you cannot force me to go, for you are virtuous, and I become more pleasing to the gods every moment I stay beside you."

Yama was delighted, and told Savitri that, for her good sense, she might obtain another boon from him.

"Then grant that my father-in-law may regain his former kingdom," she said. Yama assented and told her for the third time to go back and find her husband's body before it was devoured by jackals.

"It does not matter," said Savitri, "if the jackals devour the corpse. Of what use is the body without the soul? Another body can be found for the soul, if it is released from your noose, but never another soul for the body."

"You speak with more wisdom than most mortals," said the god. "Yet one more boon will I grant you."

"Grant me a hundred sons, oh mighty Yama," cried Savitri. And when the god bowed his head in assent, she laughed and clapped her hands. "If you are indeed a god who keeps his word with men, then release the soul of Satyavan. There is no other man that I can marry, and only by bringing him back to life can you grant me the sons you have promised!"

Yama realised that Savitri had been allowed, by a greater power than he, to triumph over him; so he loosened the coil of rope, and Satyavan's soul flew up into the air and back to the forest where his body lay. Some time later, Savitri reached the same place and found her husband lying just as she had left him.

She lifted his head, and he opened his eyes and stretched himself and yawned.

"I must have fallen asleep," he said. "Why did you not wake me before? It is almost sunset."

Hand in hand they walked home, and on the way she told him all that had happened. And when they came home they found their father and mother rejoicing with the other hermits because the old man's sight had suddenly been restored. And even as they rejoiced a messenger arrived to say that the king's enemy had been slain and that the people wished their former ruler to return to them.

The next day Savitri and Satyavan, with their parents, returned to Shalwa, and there they all lived happily for the rest of their lives. We are told that Savitri and Satyavan lived together for four hundred years, and that they had a hundred sons, as Yama had promised.

Today, when anyone in India wishes to pay a wife the highest compliment, it is said that she is like Savitri, who brought back her husband's soul from the edge of the world.

The Cow of Plenty

THERE was a wonderful cow called Surabhi, who belonged to the sage Vasishtha. The cow gave her fortunate owner anything that he wanted: food and drink, clothes and even luxuries. Whenever her owner said the word *Give*, the cow was there to give him the thing he desired. It was not surprising that jealousy and greed were roused in the hearts of those who saw or heard of this wonderful creature.

It so happens that a powerful king, Vishwamitra, was on a hunting expedition which brought him, with many of his followers, to the hermitage of Vasishtha. The holy man greeted the king with great courtesy, then called upon the cow to produce a sumptuous feast for his guests. Immediately food and drink issued from the cow in an endless stream.

The king was delighted. But he felt envious too. And soon he was asking himself why a hermit in the forest should possess such a splendid creature. It would be more reasonable, he thought, if the cow were in his own hands to provide him with his many needs.

"I'll give you ten thousand cows in exchange for this one," he told the sage.

When Vasishtha refused to listen to the proposal, the king offered him his entire kingdom.

The sage refused this generous offer, saying that the cow not only supplied him with his own necessities, but also served a similar purpose for the gods and the spirits of the dead.

"Don't forget that I am a king," said Vishwamitra, "and when kings can't have what they want, they take it by force."

"It is not for me to resist," said the sage. "I am only a hermit and a scholar. My life is devoted to the study of the sacred books. I cannot set myself against the might of your armed men. Kings do what they like, and take what they want, and never give it a moment's thought."

The king grew impatient, put a rope round the cow's neck, and began to lead her away.

Surabhi was very unwilling to go. She turned her soft, pathetic eyes towards the sage and refused to move. The king struck her several times with a stick.

At first the sage said nothing. Then he spoke to the cow: "My dear and loving Surabhi, I understand your feelings, and I do not wish to lose you. But what can I do? The king is all-powerful. He is taking you away by force and I cannot prevent him."

When the cow heard these words she broke away from her captor and came running to the sage.

"Do you wish me to go?" she cried. "Have you lost all affection for me? Do you not care whether the king ill-treats me or not? Have you given me up completely?"

"What can I say?" said the sage. "A warrior's strength lies in the force at his command. A hermit's strength lies in the spirit of forgiveness he shows. I cannot stop him from taking you, but I certainly do not abandon you or wish you to go."

"I won't be taken by force," said the cow. "If you say you want me with you, that is enough!"

As she spoke, her whole appearance underwent an amazing change. Her eyes flashed fire. Her head and neck grew to an enormous size, and she rushed at the king and his followers. Even more wonderful, great showers of burning coals poured from her tail, and the coals were followed by troops of soldiers. They came not only from her tail, but from her udder and her sides, and from the froth of her mouth. These warriors belonged to many countries and races of men – Greeks, Huns, Scythians, Parthians, Chinese – and they all wore the garments and carried the weapons peculiar to their country.

As they poured forth, they attacked the king and his men with great fury. But they inflicted no injury on them. They were content to give them a good fright. Although they chased Vishwamitra and his men for a distance of seventy-five miles, they did not kill any of them.

By the time the king had recovered his breath, he was already a changed man. He had boasted that kings could do as they liked. But now he realised that kings were really feeble compared with men of wisdom and piety. So he gave up his kingdom and went to live in a forest. He decided that he would persuade the gods to make him one of their priests. And finally, after many years of hardship, prayer and meditation, he achieved his goal and became a true sage.

King Bharata

1

Bharata and the Deer

KING BHARATA ruled over all the world. He was a thoughtful and religious man, and he looked upon the whole world as evidence of the supreme spirit of God.

He worshipped God in the form of Vishnu, the Preserver, and was full of devotion, ruling the earth for one hundred thousand years. He had five sons, amongst whom he divided all his kingdom, and went at last into the forests near the river Gandak, where he lived alone, praying and meditating.

His worship consisted of offering fresh flowers, tender leaves, and wild fruits and roots. He controlled all his senses and never grew weary. There was no one to disturb him, no one to take his mind off the worship of God. He bathed three times a day, and worshipped Vishnu in the golden sun.

One day, while Bharata was bathing in the river, he heard a lion roaring, and saw a deer, which was about to give birth to a fawn, fleeing from the lion and splashing across the river. As it reached the other side it gave birth to the fawn, and then died. Bharata saw the helpless little fawn struggling in the water. Being moved with compassion, he took it in his hands and saved it. Then he took the fawn home and cared for it, and soon began to love it. He became so attached to it that little by little he began

27

neglecting his services to God; but he was quite unaware that this was happening.

"There is no one to care for this deer," he said to himself, "and so I will look after it and bring it up. The great teachers say that to help the helpless is a virtue."

His love for the deer grew, and he used to bring it tender grass to eat, and he would bathe it, and keep it near him. Sometimes he would hold it in his arms or on his lap. He loved its company. Often, when performing some ceremony, he would break off in the middle to look for the deer.

But one day the deer disappeared.

Bharata was overcome with grief and a terrible sense of loss.

"Did I not take care of you in every way?" he mused. "Now I do not know if some animal has killed you, or if you will one day return to gladden my heart. I remember how you used to touch me gently with your horns as I sat in meditation. I remember how you would playfully trample on the things I brought for worship, and if I spoke to you in anger, you would stand at a distance till I called you again. The other hermits looked upon you as a holy animal. Perhaps the moon has taken you."

Unable to get over his sorrow, he neglected the religious ceremonies he usually performed. He had renounced his family and his kingdom in order to obtain the spiritual freedom of the hermit. Now, because of his attachment to the deer, all his strivings appeared to have been futile.

Then one day the deer returned.

Bharata was overcome with joy. He treated it as though it were his own son, and devoted the rest of his days to its welfare.

In his last days, on his death-bed, his thoughts were only of the deer; and so, upon his soul leaving his body, he was re-born as a deer. But the memory of his past life remained with him. He felt sorry that he had neglected his duties to God, and regretted his former attachment to the deer. He did not mingle with the rest of the herd, and at last left them and went away alone to his old place, where he had formerly lived and worshipped; and there he remained, bathing in the river and grazing on its banks; and so much did he desire to be freed from the body of a deer that, when he died, he was able to be born again into a Brahmin family.

2
Bharata As A Brahmin

Born to a Brahmin father, Bharata was well brought up; but remembering his former lives, he kept aloof from other people, so that many thought he was half-witted. When his parents died, his brother forced him to do menial work. People made fun of him, but he paid no attention, and took everything that came his way, good and bad. He cared neither for cold nor heat, going without clothes and sleeping on the bare ground, so that his sacred thread became black with dirt.

In spite of these hardships, he remained sturdy and strong.

One day the king of the country decided to offer a human sacrifice to the Goddess Kali, and hearing from his servants that Bharata was a useless fellow, seized him as being perfectly suitable for the sacrifice.

After a ceremonial bath, Bharata was given fine clothes and decorated with jewels. He was given rich food. Burning camphor and perfumes were placed before him. Then, accompanied by dancers and musicians, he was taken to the temple of Kali.

At the temple the king himself led Bharata to a raised platform. Sword in hand, he was about to cut off Bharata's head, when Kali, seeing Bharata and recognising him immediately as a man of God – a man without hatred in his heart, and with love for all living creatures – was afraid to receive such a sacrifice.

The goddess grew angry with the king. She became visible, and so terrifying was her aspect that the king and his followers fell dead on the spot.

Then Kali turned to Bharata and said, "No deity will allow any harm to come to you."

She disappeared, and Bharata, who feared neither the sword nor Kali, remained standing, his mind steadfast in God.

The people who had gathered to watch the sacrifice became greatly afraid. They made way for Bharata, and he returned to watch the fields as before.

Shiva's Anger

WHEN the great God Shiva and his wife Uma were sitting one day on the top of a mountain, the goddess happened to notice that the other gods and their wives were setting off together on an expedition.

"Do you know where they are going?" she asked.

"Yes," said Shiva, "they are going to attend a sacrifice that is being celebrated by Daksha, one of the Great Sages."

"But if the gods are to be there, why are you not going?" she asked. "You are the greatest of the gods. Why have you not been invited?"

"Oh, it's an old story," said Shiva. "A long time ago the gods made an agreement among themselves that I was to take no part in any of the sacrifices."

Uma was very angry to hear this. She said it was a strange arrangement that sought to exclude the most powerful of the gods. Indeed she was so upset that she said she would not speak to her husband until he took steps to alter such an unjust arrangement. Her attitude made Shiva realise that he must do something. So he got up and, calling upon all his great powers of yoga, hurried to the place where the sacrifice was being held.

Shiva was followed by thousands of demigods, whom he had called into existence, and on his behalf they put out the fires, threw down the sacrificial stakes, ate up many of those who were celebrating the sacrifice, and insulted the wives of the gods.

Lakes of milk were spilt, and mountains of dishes, containing food of every kind, were scattered far and wide.

The sacrifice itself, in the form of a deer, took refuge in flight.

Shiva was very angry when he saw the sacrifice running away, and he set off in swift pursuit.

As he ran, a drop of perspiration formed on his brow. And where it fell to the ground, a great fire sprang up. From the fire a terrible-looking creature emerged: goblin-like, with blood-red eyes and a green beard. It pursued the fleeing deer, caught up with it, and then simply gobbled it up.

Having consumed the sacrifice, the creature turned upon the gods and sages, who fled for safety in all directions. Then Brahma, the Creator, intervened, and asked Shiva to recall the terrible beast that his anger had produced, assuring him that if he did so, the gods would, in future, invite him to the celebration of every sacrifice.

Shiva agreed, but the problem now was to deal with the creature that he had brought into being. If it remained as it was, it was capable of destroying half the world. Brahma suggested that they divide the creature into a number of different parts, and so reduce its strength. Shiva agreed, and the creature was divided into many parts, and under the name of Fever those parts continue to live among beasts and men.

Fever works in different ways, and shows itself in many diseases and ailments. But Fever was originally the anger which was produced by Shiva at Daksha's sacrifice.

Nala and Damayanti

LONG AGO there reigned in Berar a famous king named Bhima. His chief claim to fame was that he had a beautiful daughter named Damayanti. She was waited upon day and night by a band of handmaids of great beauty, but she shone among them like the moon among the stars, and her hand was sought, we are told, by both gods and mortals.

Nala, King of Nishada, came to hear of Damayanti's loveliness and her many accomplishments, and was struck with passion for her. She, in turn, had heard that Nala was brave and handsome, well-read and skilled in arms. They loved each other upon the mere fame of their respective virtues, and Damayanti pined for the presence of her unknown lover.

One day while Nala was seated in a grove, dreaming of his beloved, he saw a flock of swans, with wings all flecked with gold, come to rest close by him.

Nala crept up to the leader of the flock and seized him.

"O mighty king," said the swan, "set me free, and I will do your bidding, whatever it might be."

"If a bird can do a mortal any service," said Nala, "fly to my love, Damayanti, and tell her how much I love her!" He released the bird, and it flew off to Berar, rejoicing in its freedom.

When the bird arrived in King Bhima's kingdom, it found Damayanti reclining in her garden, surrounded by her charming handmaids.

33

"What a lovely bird!" she cried when she saw the swan. "And look at its wings, all edged with gold!"

The swan came close to her and allowed itself to be made captive.

"Sweet princess," said the swan, "I come to you as a messenger of love from Nala, King of Nishada. He is as wonderful to look upon as the God of Love, and has no equal amongst mortals. The union of such a youth and maiden would be a union of perfection."

Damayanti was struck with wonder at the bird's story, and she set him free, saying, "Sweet bird! Speak to Nala on my behalf in like manner." And the swan flew back to Nala with an answering message of love.

Before long a *Swayamvara* was held for Damayanti.

This was an ancient Hindu rite by which a princess might choose her husband from an assembly of suitors come from all parts to take their chance in the selection. The heroes submitted themselves in silent rivalry to inspection as the princess walked along their line to select from the throng the favoured suitor by presenting him with a garland, or a cup of water, or some such token of regard.

Many were the princes who came to woo Damayanti, attracted by the stories of her beauty. More wonderful still, some of the gods, equally enamoured of her charms, came down to earth to woo her. Most prominent among them were the four great guardians of the world: Indra, God of Heaven; Agni, God of Fire; Varuna, God of the Waters; and Yama, God of Death. What chance did Nala, a mere mortal, have in this assembly?

Damayanti stepped into the *Swayamvara* hall, bejewelled from head to foot, bearing a garland of flowers to place round the neck of the one she would choose for her husband. She was taken round to each of the assembled princes, until she came to where her lover, Nala, was seated; but great was her dismay when she saw not one but five Nalas, each indistinguishable from the other! The gods had assumed his shape to baffle her.

But Damayanti, garland in hand, did not pause for long. She had noticed that the gods cast no shadows, because they were spirits; and that their eyes never winked, because they were the ever-wakeful Guardian Gods; and that their garlands were fresher than most, being woven of the unfading blooms of Heaven. By these tokens did Damayanti tell the gods from her lover; and she threw her garland round the neck of her beloved, the real Nala.

Then, turning to the gods, she said: "Forgive me, O mighty gods, that I have not chosen my husband from among you. I have long since pledged my heart to this prince, and the vow so pledged is sacred. Forgive me, therefore, for choosing an earthly lord and not one of the rulers of Heaven."

In this way did Damayanti, the lovely, the peerless, choose Nala for her husband, with the gods themselves as witnesses.

The happy pair then did homage before the gods, and these great guardians of the earth bestowed upon them divine blessings in reward for their constancy.

The Superior Man

JAJALI was a famous ascetic – one who practised extreme self-discipline. He had a thorough knowledge of the Vedas, most ancient of sacred books, and attended to the sacrificial fires. He observed long fasts. During the rainy season he slept under the open sky by night and lay in water by day.

In the hot weather Jajali did not seek protection from either the burning sun or the scorching wind. He slept in the most uncomfortable places, and smeared his body and long, unkempt hair with filth and mud. If he wore any clothes at all, they were made of rags and skins. He travelled over the whole earth, and dwelt in forests, mountains, or by the shores of the ocean. Once, when he was beside the ocean, he decided to conceal himself beneath its waters. He was able to do so by means of the great self-discipline which he had learnt. He could also project his mind in every direction and make himself aware of all that was happening in different parts of the world.

As Jajali lay one day at the bottom of the ocean, thinking of how his mind could travel everywhere, pride filled his heart, and he told himself that there was nobody quite like him in all the world. As he made this boast, a voice spoke in his ear. It was the voice of a spirit who had been watching him.

"You should not have made that boast, most noble Brahmin. There is a shopkeeper I know, a very virtuous man, who lives in Benares and earns a living by buying and selling perfumes. Some say he is the most virtuous of men, but I don't think he would boast about it!"

"A shopkeeper!" said the ascetic. "I should like to see this wonderful shopkeeper. Tell me where he lives, and how to get there."

The spirit gave him the necessary directions, and Jajali left his watery bed and set out for Benares.

On the way he came to a forest, where he decided to spend some time practising fresh austerities. For many days he stood absolutely still. He never moved a muscle, and to all appearance was more like a pillar of stone than a man, with his great mass of filthy, dishevelled hair on top.

It was not long before two birds, in search of a place to build their nest, decided that there was no better spot than the ascetic's head. And so they built their nest in his hair, making use of leaves and grass.

In due course the nest contained a full clutch of eggs, but Jajali never moved. Pity would have prevented him from doing so. Eventually the eggs were hatched, the young birds emerged. Days passed, and their feathers grew. As more days passed, they learned to fly. Then they would go off with their parents for a few hours at a time, in search of food. By now the ascetic had really fulfilled his obligations to the welfare of his guests; but still he did not move! Once they were absent for a week, but he waited until they returned. Finally, he waited for a month, and when they did not come back he decided that they had abandoned the nest for ever, and that he was free to move.

Unfortunately, Jajali felt very proud of himself when he thought of his noble conduct.

"There is nobody like me in all the wide world," he said to himself. "I must have acquired a great store of merit by this unselfish act."

He felt so pleased with himself that he slapped his arms and shouted out loud, "There is noobody my equal anywhere!"

And once more he heard a voice – a voice as it seemed from heaven: "Jajali! Don't say that. You are not as good a man as the shopkeeper in Benares, and *he* would not boast as you have done."

Jajali's heart was filled with anger, and he decided that he would go to Benares without further delay and see this wonderful shopkeeper.

When he arrived in Benares, one of the first persons he saw was the shopkeeper busily engaged in his shop, buying and selling herbs and perfumes. The shopkeeper saw him and called out a welcome: "I have been expecting you, most noble Brahmin, for a long time. I have heard of your great asceticism, of how you lived immersed in the ocean, and of all that you have done since, even allowing the birds to build a nest in your hair. I know, too, of how proud you were of that, and of how a voice from heaven rebuked you. You were angry, and that is why you came here. Tell me what you want. I shall do my best to help you."

The Brahmin replied: "You are a shopkeeper, my friend, and the son of a shopkeeper. How does a person like you, who spends all his time buying and selling, acquire so much knowledge and so much wisdom? Where did you get it?"

"My knowledge and wisdom consist in nothing but this," said the shopkeeper. "I follow and obey that ancient teaching which everybody knows and which consists of universal friendliness and kindness to man and beast. I earn my livelihood by trade, but my scales are always just. I never cheat anyone, and I never injure anyone in thought, word or deed. I quarrel with no-one, fear no-one, hate no-one, praise no-one, abuse no-one. And I am convinced that the life I live is the life that secures both prosperity and heaven just as surely as the life that is devoted to penance and sacrifice."

As he proceeded, the shopkeeper became more assertive, more critical, even a little boastful! Not only did he condemn the killing of animals, he also expressed his disapproval of agriculture, because the plough gives pain to the earth and causes death of many tiny creatures living in the soil – apart from the forced labour it took from bullocks and slaves! As for animal sacrifices, he said they had been started by greedy priests. The true sacrifice was the sacrifice performed by the mind, and if there had to be sacrifices at all, people should use herbs and fruits and balls of rice. Nor did he believe in pilgrimages. There was no need to wander all over the land, visiting sacred rivers and mountains. There was no place so holy as the soul itself.

Jajali was indignant. He told the holder of the scales, as he called him, that he was an atheist! How were men to live if they did not plough the ground? Where would they get food? And as for sacrifices, the world would come to an end if we gave them up.

The shopkeeper declared that if only men would go back to the real teaching of the Vedas, they would find that there was no need to plough the ground. In ancient days the earth yielded all that was required. Herbs and plants grew of themselves.

Despite the strength of the shopkeeper's arguments, the ascetic was not convinced. We are told that both he and the shopkeeper died not long afterwards, and that each went to his own particular heaven – their heavens being as different as were their ways of life.

Shakuntala

IN ANCIENT INDIA, when the great God Indra was worshipped, there lived a young king named Dushyanta.

One day, while he was hunting in a great forest, the king became separated from his followers. He wandered on alone through the forest until he found himself in a pleasant grove which led to a hermitage. The little dwelling was the home of an old hermit called Father Kanva. The king had heard many stories about the piety and wisdom of the old man, and decided to honour him with a visit.

To the king's disappointment, however, the hermitage was empty. He turned away and was about to leave the grove when a gentle voice said, "Wait, my lord," and a girl stepped out from behind the trees.

In spite of her poor clothes, the girl was so beautiful and dignified that the king's admiration was aroused and he asked her courteously, "Isn't this the dwelling-place of holy Kanva?"

"Yes, my lord," she replied. "But my father is away on a pilgrimage. Will you not rest here a while?"

She brought him water and fruits for his refreshment, and the king was delighted at the hospitality he was shown. It was clear to him that she did not recognize him as the king: so Dushyanta, who liked to mingle unrecognised among his people, pretended to be a huntsman, and asked the girl her name.

"I am called Shakuntala," she said. "I am Father Kanva's

adopted daughter."

Encouraged to go on, she told the king that she had been left an orphan when she was very small, and that Kanva had treated her as lovingly as if he had really been her father. Though she was of noble birth, she was very happy living a simple life in the forest.

As Dushyanta listened to her and watched her beautiful face, he felt that he could linger in that enchanting spot for ever; but he knew that his followers must be anxiously searching for him, so he took leave of Shakuntala and made his way back to the hunting party.

But he did not leave the forest. Instead he ordered his men to encamp at some distance from the hermitage. The next day, and the following day as well, found him visiting Shakuntala at the hermitage.

Dushyanta and Shakuntala were soon confessing their love for each other; but when the girl learnt that it was the king himself who wished to marry her, she protested that he would surely regret such a hasty decision. Dushyanta, however, soothed her fears, and, dreading lest something might come between them, persuaded her to wed him without delay.

There was no need for a priest to marry the lovers, since, in those days, it was lawful for kings and warriors to wed their brides by a simple exchange of flowers or garlands. And so Dushyanta and Shakuntala vowed to be true to each other for ever.

"Come with me to my palace," said the king. "My people shall acknowledge you as their queen."

"I cannot leave the forest until I have told Father Kanva of our marriage," said Shakuntala. "I must wait for him to return. But you must return to your palace to carry out your duties. When you come again, I will be ready to join you."

The king placed a ring, engraven with the name "Dushyanta", upon her finger, and promised to return soon.

When he had left, Shakuntala wandered dreamily about the forest, forgetting that someone might visit the hermitage to see Father Kanva. At nightfall when she returned to the grove, she was met by a visitor who was spluttering with rage.

The visitor was an old sage named Durvasas, who was dreaded by all because of his violent temper. It was said that if anyone offended him, he would punish them severely. He was known as a "master-curser."

The sage had been waiting at the hermitage a long time, and felt that he had been insulted by Shakuntala. She pleaded for forgiveness, and begged him to stay; but the old man was in a terrible mood. Thrusting the girl aside, he hurried away muttering a curse under his breath.

Shakuntala was troubled not so much by the curse as by the feeling that she had neglected her duties; for in India it is something of a sin if one receives a visitor and allows the guest to depart unhonoured.

Then something happened which worried Shakuntala even more. Whilst she was bathing in the stream near her home, the ring, the king's gift, slipped from her finger and disappeared in the water.

Shakuntala wept bitterly at her loss; but she was not to know what heartbreak it was to bring her in the future, or how closely her bad luck was connected with the angry sage Durvasas.

It was a great relief to her when Father Kanva returned from his pilgrimage. He was not displeased at the news of her marriage to Dushyanta. On the contrary, he was overjoyed.

"My daughter, you are worthy of the king," he said. "Gladly will I give you to Dushyanta when he comes to claim you."

But the days passed, and King Dushyanta did not come.

Shakuntala felt a great weight begin to press against her heart. What could have happened? Was Dushyanta ill, or had he repented of his rash marriage? But no, she could never believe that...

Then Father Kanva, growing uneasy, said: "My daughter, since the king does not come, you must seek him in his palace. For though it grieves me to part with you, a wife's place is by her husband's side."

Dushyanta had asked her to wait for him; but she could not refuse to do Father Kanva's bidding. And so, for the first time in her life, she left her forest home and journeyed to the unknown world beyond.

After several days she reached the royal city, and, learning that the king was in his palace, she asked permission to see him, saying that she had brought a message from Father Kanva.

When she found herself at the foot of the king's throne, she looked up so that he could see her face, and said, "Do not be angry with me, my lord, but since you did not keep your promise to claim me soon, I have been forced to seek you here."

"My promise to claim you?" King Dushyanta looked bewildered. "What do you mean?"

Shakuntala looked at him with fear in her eyes.

"You are mocking me, my lord," she said. "Have you forgotten our marriage in the forest, and how you said you would cherish me for ever? Do not look so strangely at me, I beg you, but acknowledge me as your bride!"

"My bride!" exclaimed the king. "What fantasy is this? I have never seen you before!"

Shakuntala was astounded. What has happened to him? she wondered. I have always dreaded that he would repent of our hasty marriage. But surely he would not deny me? And she stretched out her arms to him and cried, "How can you say such

words? They are not worthy of a king. What have I done that you should treat me so cruelly?"

"I have never seen you before," said the king firmly. "You must be either mad or wicked to come to me with such a tale."

Shakuntala stood looking at him with growing despair in her heart. Then, realising from the king's hard countenance the hopelessness of her situation, she fled from the palace, weeping bitterly.

Now, although King Dushyanta appeared to have become callous and cruel in such a short space of time, in reality he had only spoken what he believed to be the truth. He did not remember Shakuntala at all, and for a very good reason. When the old sage Durvasas had muttered his curse, he had decreed, first of all, that she should lose the king's ring, and then, that until Dushayanta saw the ring again, he would be unable to remember Shakuntala, even though she stood before him.

Not even the God Indra could alter a curse once it had been pronounced by the old sage, and since Dushyanta's ring had been swept away by the stream in the forest, there was little hope that he would ever remember his bride.

Several years passed, and then one day a fisherman was brought before the king to relate a curious story.

The fisherman had caught a fine carp in the river, and when he had cut the fish open, a gold ring engraven with the name "Dushyanta" was found within the body of the carp.

The king examined the ring with interest. "It does look like mine," he said, "yet I don't remember losing it."

He rewarded the fisherman for his honesty, and after examining the ring again, he placed it upon his finger.

"How strange!" he said. "A cloud seems to be lifting from my mind. Yes, I remember now – this is the ring I gave to my bride,

Shakuntala, in the forest. Ah, but what have I done! It was Shakuntala who came to me that day, and I sent her from me with cruel words."

Dushyanta hastened to the forest, but the hermitage was deserted. Father Kanva was long since dead. The king had the land searched, but it was as though Shakuntala had vanished from the earth. He fell into a deep melancholy from which no one could rouse him.

But although the God Indra had not been able to avert the curse of Durvasas, he had not been indifferent to the suffering that had been caused. And now that the ring had been recovered, he was determined to help the unhappy king.

One day Dushyanta was walking in his garden when he saw a strange object in the sky. It looked like a great shining bird.

As it came nearer, the bird proved to be a chariot drawn by prancing horses, whose reins were held by a celestial-looking being.

The chariot alighted on the earth not far from the king, and the charioteer called: "Dushyanta! Do you not know me? I am Matali, the charioteer of great Indra. Come with me, for Indra has need of you."

Dushyanta was awestruck; but he stepped into the chariot and was whirled upwards so swiftly that soon his kingdom lay like a speck beneath him. The chariot soared still higher, and the horses trod the air as if it were solid ground beneath their feet. Then suddenly the chariot stopped in the midst of the clouds, and Matali told Dushyanta to descend.

The king obeyed, and gradually, as the mist cleared and the clouds melted away, he saw that he was alone in a beautiful garden. He felt that surely he was near great Indra's dwelling.

There was a rustling in the bushes, and Dushyanta waited breathlessly. Perhaps the God was about to reveal himself.

It was not a heavenly being who appeared, however, but a little boy who was carrying a lion cub. The cub struggled fiercely in his arms, but the boy held on to it without fear.

"Come here, boy," called the king. "Tell me your name."

"I do not know it," said the boy.

"That is strange," said Dushyanta. He felt irresistibly drawn towards the boy, and held out his hand to him, but the boy drew back.

"No one shall touch me," he said, and then called out: "Mother, come quickly!"

"I am coming, son," said a gentle voice.

The king stepped back, trembling violently, for there before him stood Shakuntala, looking pale and sad but more beautiful than ever.

When she saw the king she drew herself up proudly, but Dushyanta fell at her feet, crying: "Shakuntala, do not turn from me. Listen, I beg of you!" And he told her of how he had forgotten her until the recovery of the ring, and of how he had since sought her everywhere.

Shakuntala's face lit up with joy and she cried, "Oh, Dushyanta, now I undertand. It must have been the punishment of Durvasas." And she told him about the curse of the angry sage, how she had lost her ring in the stream, and how she had suffered all these years at the thought of her husband's denial of her.

"But where have you been all the time?" asked Dushyanta. "What is the place?"

"This is a sacred mountain near the dwelling-place of great Indra. When you denied me in your palace, I felt that I should die of grief. But a wonderful thing happened to me. As I lay weeping on the ground, Indra send his chariot to earth, and I was brought here by heavenly beings who have watched over us all this time."

"Mother," cried the boy, who had been watching from a little distance. "Who is this man?"

"Your father, my child," said Shakuntala. "Embrace your son, Dushyanta. He was a gift from the gods to comfort me in my loneliness."

And as Dushyanta knelt down to embrace his son, Matali again appeared in his chariot.

"Are you happy, Dushyanta?" he asked, "Now it is Indra's wish that you return with me to earth. Cherish your son, happy mortals, for he shall become the founder of a race of heroes."

The chariot took them back to earth, and from that time Dushyanta and Shakuntala lived in great happiness, while their son, whom they named Bharata, grew up to found a noble race, as Matali had foretold.

Tales from The Jataka

The Hare
in the Moon

ALONG TIME AGO, when animals could talk, there lived
in a forest four wise creatures – a hare, a jackal, an otter, and a
monkey.

They were good friends, and every evening they would sit
together in a forest glade to discuss the events of the day,
exchange advice, and make good resolutions. The hare was the
noblest and wisest of the four. He believed in the superiority of
men and women, and was always telling his friends tales of
human goodness and wisdom.

One evening, when the moon rose in the sky – and in those
days the moon's face was clear and unmarked – the hare looked
up at it carefully and said: "Tomorrow good men will observe a
fast, for I can see that it will be the middle of the month. They
will eat no food before sunset, and during the day they will give
alms to any beggar or holy man who may meet them. Let us
promise to do the same. In that way, we can come a little closer
to human beings in dignity and wisdom."

The others agreed, and then went their different ways.

Next day, the otter got up, stretched himself, and was
preparing to get his breakfast when he remembered the vow he
had taken with his friends.

If I keep my word, how hungry I shall be by evening! he
thought. I'd better make sure that there's plenty to eat once the
fast is over. He set off towards the river.

A fisherman had caught several large fish early that morning, and had buried them in the sand, planning to return for them later. The otter soon smelt them out.

"A supper all ready for me!" he said to himself. "But since it's a holy day, I mustn't steal." Instead he called out: "Does anyone own this fish?"

There being no answer, the otter carried the fish off to his home, setting it aside for his evening meal. Then he locked his front door and slept all through the day, undisturbed by beggars or holy men asking for alms.

Both the monkey and the jackal felt much the same way when they got up that morning. They remembered their vows but thought it best to have something put by for the evening. The jackal found some stale meat in someone's back yard. Ah, that should improve with age, he thought, and took it home for his evening meal. And the monkey climbed a mango tree and picked a bunch of mangoes. Like the otter, they decided to sleep through the day.

The hare woke early. Shaking his long ears, he came out of his burrow and sniffed the dew-drenched grass.

When evening comes, I can have my fill of grass, he thought. But if a beggar or holy man comes my way, what can I give him? I cannot offer him grass, and I have nothing else to give. I shall have to offer myself. Most men seem to relish the flesh of the hare. We're good to eat, I'm told. And pleased with this solution to the problem, he scampered off.

Now the God Sakka had been resting on a cloud not far away, and he had heard the hare speaking aloud.

"I will test him," said the god. "Surely no hare can be so noble and unselfish."

Towards evening, God Sakka descended from his cloud, and assuming the form of an old priest, he sat down near the hare's burrow. When the animal came home from his romp, he said: "Good evening, little hare. Can you give me something to eat? I have been fasting all day, and am so hungry that I cannot pray."

The hare, remembering his vow, said: "Is it true that men enjoy eating the flesh of the hare?"

"Quite true," said the priest.

"In that case," said the hare, "since I have no other food to offer you, you can make a meal of me."

"But I am a holy man, and this is a holy day, and I may not kill any living creature with my own hands."

"Then collect some dry sticks and set them alight. I will leap into the flames myself, and when I am roasted you can eat me."

God Sakka marvelled at these words, but he was still not quite convinced, so he caused a fire to spring up from the earth. The hare, without any hesitation, jumped into the flames.

"What's happening?" called the hare after a while. "The fire surrounds me, but not a hair of my coat is singed. In fact, I'm feeling quite cold!"

As the hare spoke, the fire died down, and he found himself sitting on the cool sweet grass. Instead of the old priest, there stood before him the God Sakka in all his radiance.

"I am God Sakka, little hare, and having heard your vow, I wanted to test your sincerity. Such unselfishness of yours deserves immortality. It must be known throughout the world."

God Sakka then stretched out his hand towards the mountain, and drew from it some of the essence which ran in its veins. This he threw towards the moon, which had just risen, and instantly the outline of the hare appeared on the moon's surface.

Then leaving the hare in a bed of sweet grass, he said: "For ever and ever, little hare, you shall look down from the moon upon the world, to remind men of the old truth, 'Give to others, and the gods will give to you.'"

The Ugly Prince and the
Heartless Princess

IN THE KINGDOM OF MALLA there was once a young prince named Kusa, who was famed for his great kindness and wisdom; but unfortunately he was very ugly.

In spite of his ugliness, everyone in the kingdom was extremely fond of the prince; but Kusa himself was sensitive about his appearance, and when his father, King Okkaka, urged him to marry, he said: "Don't ask me to get married. How could a beautiful princess love such an ugly fellow?"

But the king insisted, and at last Kusa grew so tired of refusing to choose a bride, that he hit upon a scheme by which he hoped to free himself for ever from the problem of his marriage. He was very skilful with his hands, and he fashioned a golden image, and showing the king his handiwork, he said: "If a princess as beautiful as this image can be found for me, I will make her my bride. Otherwise I will remain single."

Kusa felt sure that there was no princess who could compare with his statue; but the king was determined to find such a beauty, and he sent messengers far and wide.

The messengers visited many kingdoms, carrying the statue with them. Whenever they arrived at a city or a village, they asked the inhabitants whether they knew of anyone who resembled the golden image. But nowhere was such a beauty to be found until the messengers reached the kingdom of Madda.

The King of Madda had eight lovely daughters, and the eldest of them, Pabhavati, bore an extraordinary resemblance to the golden image. When the messengers saw her, they went straight to the king and said that they had come to ask the hand of Princess Pabhavati for Prince Kusa, the son of King Okkaka.

The King of Madda knew that Okkaka was a rich and powerful king, and he was pleased at the idea of being allied to him through marriage.

"If King Okkaka will visit me," he said, "I will give him the hand of Princess Pabhavati for his son, Prince Kusa."

The messengers hurried back to Malla with the good news, and King Okkaka was delighted at the outcome of their mission; but poor Kusa was dismayed.

"But my dear Father," he said to the king, "how will such a beautiful princess behave when she sees how ugly I am? She will surely flee from me at once."

"Do not worry, my son," said King Okkaka. "I will revive an ancient custom in order to protect you. According to this custom, a bride may not look upon the face of her husband until one year after the marriage. Therefore, for one whole year, you must only meet your bride in a darkened room."

"But how will that help me in the end?" asked Kusa doubtfully. "My looks will not have improved by the end of the year. She will have to see me some day."

"True, but during that year your bride will have learned to love you so much that, when she sees you at last, you will not be ugly in her eyes!"

Prince Kusa still had his doubts, but the king was insistent and wasted no time in visiting the kingdom of Madda and returning with the beautiful Princess Pabhavati. Soon after, the marriage ceremony was performed in a darkened chamber, by order of the king.

Princess Pabhavati was surprised to discover that she was not to look upon the face of her husband for one year after the marriage had taken place.

This is a strange custom, she thought, but she accepted the condition without protest, and settled down in a magnificent suite of apartments, one room of which was always to be kept in complete darkness.

Kusa came daily to this room to visit his bride, and as his voice and manners were kind and gentle, Pabhavati soon grew to love him, although she did not get a glimpse of his face. He spent many hours playing to her upon his *sitar*, and she would listen to him, enthralled.

Was there ever a prince like this husband of mine? she thought. How I long for the day when I shall see his face! Surely he must be as handsome as he is kind and wise.

All might have been well if Pabhavati had been content to wait for a year; but, after she had been married for only a month, she grew impatient and found herself constantly wondering about Prince Kusa's appearance. During the second month she could conceal her curiosity no longer. One day, when Kusa was with her in the darkened room, she said: "Dear husband, it makes me sad that I must wait so long before I can look upon your face. I beg you to meet me in the light of day."

"No, Pabhavati, that is impossible," said the prince. "I cannot disobey my father the king. Be patient a little longer. The months will pass quickly."

But the quality of patience was absent in the princess, and soon she began to question the maidservants and others about her husband's appearance. As she never received a clear answer, she became even more curious. Finally she bribed one of her attendants to help her obtain a glimpse of Kusa.

One day, when the Prince was due to ride through the city at the head of a procession, the waiting-woman concealed the princess in a corner-room of the palace, a window of which looked out upon the highway.

When the procession came by, Pabhavati hurried to the window. She heard the sound of music and shouting, and saw gay banners and garlands thrown at the feet of the elephant upon which Prince Kusa was riding in state.

"Long live Kusa, our noble prince!" cried the people on the streets.

As the elephant passed beneath the window, Pabhavati caught a glimpse of the prince's face. She shrank back in horror.

"Oh, no!" she cried. "Can that hideous creature be my husband? No, that is not Kusa!"

Her attendant assured her that it was indeed the prince, whereupon Pabhavati decided that she would flee instantly from such an ugly husband. She demanded that an escort be provided for her return to the kingdom of Madda, declaring that she would not be bound by marriage to a husband who was so different from the man she had imagined!

King Okkaka could have forced the princess to remain in the palace, but Kusa shook his head sadly and said, "No, let her do as she wishes."

Then, forgetful of all the love and tenderness that she had received from Kusa, and thinking only of his ugly face, Pabhavati left the palace and returned to her father's kingdom.

Prince Kusa was terribly unhappy; but one day the thought occurred to him that if he were to visit Pabhavati in her own land, he might find that her attitude had changed. He changed his princely robes for simple clothes, and, taking his *sitar*, he set out on foot for the kingdom of Madda.

After a journey of several days, Kusa arrived one evening at the chief city of Madda.

It was midnight when he reached the royal palace. He crept

beneath the walls, then began playing softly upon his *sitar*. He played so sweetly that the sleepers in the palace stirred and smiled in their dreams. But Pabhavati wakened with a start and tensed as she listened to the familiar music.

That is Kusa below, she thought, afraid and angry at the same time. If my father knows that he is here, I will be forced to return to that hideous husband.

But Kusa had no intention of appealing to the king. He would rather lose Pabhavati for ever than have her return against her will. He was determined to keep his presence in the city a secret from everyone except the princess.

When morning came he went to the chief potter in the city and asked to become his apprentice.

"If I do good work for you, will you display my wares in the palace?" asked Kusa.

"Certainly," said the potter. "But show me what you can do."

Kusa set to work at the potter's wheel, and the bowls he produced were so beautifully formed that the potter was delighted.

"I am sure the king will purchase such dainty bowls for his daughters," he said; and taking some of the bowls made by Kusa, he went straight to the palace.

The King took a great fancy to the potter's new wares. When he learned that they had been made by a new apprentice, he said: "Give the young man a thousand gold pieces, and tell him that from now on he must work only for my daughters. Now take eight of these beautiful bowls to the princesses as my gifts to them."

The potter did as he was told, and the king's daughters were thrilled with their presents; but Pabhavati knew in her heart that they had been fashioned by Kusa. She returned her bowl to the potter and said, "Take this bowl back to your apprentice and tell

him that it is as ugly as he is."

When the potter passed on these remarks to Kusa, the prince sighed and thought: How can I touch her hard heart? If I could speak to her, it might make a difference. Tomorrow I will seek service in the palace.

He gave the potter the king's gold pieces and said goodbye; then, hearing that the palace cook needed an assistant, he presented himself at the royal kitchens.

The cook took Kusa into his service, and the prince proved to be as good a cook as he was a potter – so much so, that a dish specially prepared by him was sent straight to the king.

The king thoroughly enjoyed the dish, and when he heard that it had been prepared by the cook's new assistant, he said: "Give him a thousand pieces of gold, and from now on let him prepare and serve all the food for myself and my daughters."

Kusa was happy to give the king's gold piece to the chief cook, then set to work to prepare a delicious meal.

At dinner, Pabhavati was horrified to see her husband, disguised as a cook, stagger into the banquet-hall with a heavy load of dishes. He gave no sign of recognition; but the princess was angry and, staring at him with contempt, said: "I do not care for these dishes. Bring me food that someone else has prepared."

Her sisters protested, crying out that they had never tasted such delicious cooking. But although Kusa came day after day, serving a variety of tasty dishes, Pabhavati would not touch any of them.

At last the prince decided that there was no way in which he could touch the heart of the princess.

Nothing that I do pleases her, he thought. Now I must leave her for ever.

While he was preparing to leave the palace, he heard that the King of Madda was greatly troubled. The king had received news that seven kings were riding towards the city with seven armies, and that each of these kings, having heard of the beauty of Pabhavati, was anxious to make her his wife.

The king was in a quandary, because he felt sure that if he chose one of these kings as the husband of Pabhavati, the other six would attack his kingdom in revenge.

If only Pabhavati had not left her rightful husband, thought the king, these troubles would not have arisen.

Realising that it was useless to spend his time in regrets, the king summoned his advisers and asked them which king he should choose for the princess.

"Not one of them alone," declared the wise men. "The princess has endangered the kingdom. Therefore she must suffer the consequences. She must be executed, her body divided into seven pieces, and one portion presented to each of the seven kings. Only in this way can a terrible war be avoided."

The king was horrified by this advice from his men of wisdom; but while he was sitting alone, deep in thought, Kusa, still in the guise of a cook, came to him and said: "Your majesty, let me deal with these kings. Give me your army, and I will crush them or die in the attempt."

"What!" cried the astonished king. "Shall a cook do battle with kings?"

"If a cook knows how to fight, why not? But I must confess that I am not really a servant, but Prince Kusa, to whom you once entrusted your daughter. Although she has rejected me, I still love her, and it is only right that I should deal with these suitors."

The king could hardly believe that it was Kusa who stood before him. He had Pabhavati brought to him, and when she admitted that the cook's apprentice was her royal husband, he cried: "You should be ashamed, daughter, for allowing your husband to be treated as a servant in the palace."

He dismissed Pabhavati from his presence, and begged Kusa's pardon for the way in which he had been insulted.

Kusa replied that all he wanted was freedom to deal with the seven invading kings, and the king immediately placed him at the head of an army. The fate of the kingdom lay in Kusa's hands.

The seven kings were taken by surprise when they saw Kusa and his forces advancing towards them, for they had not expected any resistance. In spite of their superior numbers, they were soon routed by an inspired force under Kusa's command. They laid down their arms and surrendered, and the Prince led them as captives to the king.

"Deal with these prisoners as you will," said Kusa.

"They are your captives," said the king. "It is for you to decide their fate."

"Then," said the prince, "since each of these kings wishes to marry a beautiful princess, why do you not marry them all to the sisters of Pabhavati?"

The king was delighted with this solution to his problem; it would guarantee the safety of his kingdom for ever. The seven kings were bowled over by the beauty and grace of Pabhavati's sisters. And the seven sisters thought their prospective husbands looked very handsome indeed.

But Pabhavati sat alone, weeping bitter tears. She now realised how heartlessly she had treated Kusa, and what a noble man and lover she had scorned.

He will never forgive me, she thought sadly.

She went to him, and threw herself at his feet, crying: "Forgive me, my husband, and take me back, even if you decide to treat me as a slave."

Kusa raised her gently from the ground.

"Do you really wish to return to me?" he asked. "Look at me,

Pabhavati. I am still as ugly as when you ran away from me."

Pabhavati gazed at him steadfastly; and instead of the loathing which Kusa had seen in her eyes before, he now saw only wonder and tenderness.

"You have changed!" she cried. "You are no longer ugly!"

"No," said Kusa. "I haven't changed. It is you who have changed."

The Crane
and the Crab

EVERY SUMMER the water in the village pond fell very low, and one could see the fish swimming about near the bottom. A crane caught sight of them and said to himself, "I must find a way to get hold of those fish." And he sat down in deep thought by the side of the pond.

When the fish caught sight of the crane, they said, "Of what are you thinking, my lord, as you sit there?"

"I am thinking about you," said the crane. "The water in this pool being very low, the heat so great, and food so very scarce, I was wondering what in the world you fishes were going to do!"

"And what do you suggest we do, sir?"

"Well, if you agree, I will take you up one by one in my beak, and carry you off to a fine large pool covered with five different kinds of lotus-flowers, and there I will put you down."

"But, good sir," they said, "no crane ever took the slightest thought for the welfare of a fish ever since the world began. Your desire is to eat us, one by one."

"No, I will not eat you while you trust me," said the crane. "If you don't take my word that there is such a pool, send one of your number to go with me and see for himself."

Believing this to be a fair proposal, the fish presented the crane with a great big fish (blind in one eye), who they thought would be a match for the crane whether on land or water. The crane carried the fish off and dropped him in the pool, and after allowing him to take a good look at it, brought him back to his old pond. Then he told all the other fish about the charms of the new pool.

The fish became eager to go there, and said to the crane, "We shall be grateful, my lord, if you would kindly take us across."

Well, to begin with, the crane took the big one-eyed fish again and carried him off to the new pool; but instead of dropping the fish in the water, the crane alighted in a tree which grew at the edge of the pool. Dashing the fish down in a fork of the tree, the crane pecked it to death. He then picked it clean and let the bones fall at the foot of the tree.

When the crane returned to the pond, he said, "I've thrown him in. Who's next?"

And so he took the fish one by one, and ate them all. But there was still a crab remaining in the muddy waters of the pond. And the crane wanted to eat him too.

"Mister crab," he said, "I've carried all those fine fish away and dropped them into a beautiful large pool. Come along, I'll take you there too."

"And how will you carry me across?" asked the crab.

"In my beak, of course."

"Ah, but you might drop me like that." And to himself he said: "He hasn't put the fish in the pool, that's certain. But if he would really put me in, it would be wonderful. I could do with a change. And, if he *doesn't* – well, I think I know how to deal with him!" And he spoke to the crane: "You won't be able to hold me tight enough, friend crane. But we crabs have a very firm grip. If I might take hold of your neck with my claws, I could hold on tight and go along with you."

The crane agreed, and the crab took hold of the bird's neck with his pincers, and said, "Let's go." The crane flew him across and showed him the pool, and then started off for the tree.

"You're going the wrong way, friend," said the crab.

"Don't call me friend," said the crane. "I suppose you thought me your slave to lift you up and carry you about! Well, just take a look at that heap of bones at the foot of the tree. As I ate up all those fish, so I will eat you too."

"It was because of their own foolishness that the fish were eaten," said the crab. "I won't be giving you the same opportunity. If we die, we will die together." And he tightened his grip on the crane's long neck.

With his mouth open and the tears streaming from his eyes, the crane gasped, "Lord, indeed I will not eat you! Spare my life!"

"Well then, just step down to the pool and put me in," said the crab.

The crane turned back to the pool, and placed the crab in the mud at the water's edge.

"Thank you, friend," said the crab, and nipped off the crane's head as neatly as if he were cutting a lotus-stalk with a knife.

Friends in Deed

AN ANTELOPE lived in a thicket near a small lake. Not far from the lake, a woodpecker had her nest at the top of a tree. And in the lake lived a tortoise. The three became friends, and lived together very happily.

A hunter, wandering about in the forest, noticed the antelope's footprints at the edge of the water; and he set a trap for it, made of leather thongs, and then went his way. That night the antelope went down to the lake to drink, and got caught in the noose. He cried aloud for help. Hearing him, the woodpecker flew down from her tree-top, and the tortoise came out of the water, and they consulted each other about what to do.

Said the woodpecker, "Friend tortoise, you have teeth to bite through the snare. I will go and see to it that the hunter stays away. If we both do our best, our friend will not lose his life."

The tortoise began to gnaw the leather thong, and the woodpecker made her way to the hunter's dwelling. At day-break, the hunter came out, knife in hand. As soon as the bird saw him, she cried out, flapped her wings, and struck him in the face as he walked out of his front door.

"A bird of ill omen has struck me!" muttered the hunter, and he turned back and remained indoors for a while. Then he got ready again, and picked up his hunting-knife.

The woodpecker reasoned, "The first time he came out by the front door, now he will leave by the back." And she settled on a fence behind the house. Sure enough, the hunter came out by the back, and the bird cried out again and struck him in the face.

"An unlucky bird for certain!" exclaimed the hunter. "The creature will not leave me alone." Turning back, he stayed at home till next day, when he picked up his knife and started out again.

The woodpecker hurried back to her friends. "Here comes the hunter!" she cried. By this time the tortoise had gnawed through all the thongs but one. His teeth felt as though they would fall out, and his mouth was sore and smeared with blood. The antelope saw the young hunter running through the clearing, knife in hand. Making a great effort, he burst through the last thong, and fled into the woods. The woodpecker flew to the top of a tall tree. But the tortoise was so weak that he lay where he was; and the hunter threw him into a bag, and tied it to the tree.

When the antelope saw that the tortoise had been captured, he was determined to save his friend's life. So he let the hunter see him, and pretended to be weak and lame. The hunter saw him, seized his knife, and set off in pursuit. The antelope, keeping just out of his reach, led him into the forest; and when he judged that they had come a sufficient distance, he gave the hunter the slip and returned swiftly by another way. Then he lifted the bag with his horns, dropped it on the ground, ripped it open and let the tortoise out. And the woodpecker came down from the tree.

Then the antelope spoke to his friends: "You have been true friends and have saved my life. Now the hunter will come after you. So you, friend woodpecker, must move elsewhere in the forest with your brood. And you, friend tortoise, must dive into the water and take up residence on the other side of the lake."

So they went their different ways, and when the hunter returned, he could find none of them. He picked up his torn bag, and went home feeling sorry for himself.

"Who'll Buy My Mangoes?"

WHEN IT WAS KNOWN that the King of Benares was anxious to marry, kings and princes came from different corners of the country to propose that he marry their daughters. But he would choose none of them. If the daughters were acceptable, their parents were not; and so, when they had all gone, the king sat gloomily at his window, wondering if he would ever find someone to his liking.

His window looked out on the market-place. The bazaar was busy and colourful, fruit-sellers and cloth-merchants and bangle-makers displaying their wares on the pavements. The humbler tradespeople made their way through the crowds, and their voices, shouting their wares, rose harshly in the air. Amongst these voices the king could distinguish one – clear and musical – calling, "Mangoes! Who'll buy my mangoes?"

The voice pleased him, and the king's gaze roved over the crowd until he found its owner – Sujata, the daughter of a poor fruit-vendor, who was busily plying her trade. In spite of the ragged clothes she wore, she was a lovely girl, graceful in her movements, slim-waisted, her eyes bright and lustrous; and she was quite unconscious of her beauty.

The king's heart was smitten. Turning to one of his courtiers, he commanded him to bring the girl before him.

With downcast eyes, the innocent Sujata was led into the royal presence. The king could do nothing but gape at her.

The courtiers put their heads together and whispered, "Surely the king will not marry the daughter of a fruit-seller when he has rejected all the high-born princesses in the land!"

But that was just what the king intended. Sujata consented to wed him, and the marriage was celebrated with all the pomp and ceremony of a royal wedding.

At first the king and queen lived together in perfect harmony; but after a few months the king began to notice a disquieting change in his wife. Her natural simplicity, which had so charmed him, left her; and she became cold and haughty, especially with her servants or others of humble upbringing.

By the time they had been married for two years, the king's patience had worn thin. On their wedding anniversary he held a banquet in honour of his queen, and they sat side by side partaking of the fine dishes that were placed before them. The king talked gaily to his friends, but Sujata was in a surly mood; she sat silent and disdainful. Towards the end of the meal, bowls of fruit were placed before them – pomegranates, pears, mangoes, dates and figs.

The king, with his own hands, placed a luscious mango upon Sujata's plate.

"What is this thing?" asked the queen coldly. "Am I supposed to eat it?"

The king was astonished. "So it has come to this, has it?" he cried in anger. "You have forgotten who you were before I made you a queen. You have grown proud and scornful. I found you selling mangoes in the market-place, and to the market-place you must return! Perhaps, then, you will learn again what a mango is!"

Sujata got up without a word, and left the feast; and from that day nothing was heard of her.

The king told everyone that he did not want to see her again,

but he had not taken his feelings for her into account. As the days and weeks and months passed, life without his beautiful Sujata became unbearable. He forgot her faults and only remembered her charm and simplicity in the early days of their marriage. He sent his messengers into the city to find her and to bring her back, but she was not to be found. No one knew where she had gone.

One day the king was in another city, passing through the market-place. Amid the clamour of the bazaar his ears caught the well-known cry: "Mangoes! Who'll buy my mangoes?" And there, to his joy, was Sujata in the crowd.

She was dressed in rags, as of old. Her beauty had been dimmed through hunger and privation. But in the eyes of the king she was as lovely as ever.

Throwing a cloak across part of his face, he approached her and asked, "What have you there, girl?"

"Mangoes, fine mangoes, sir," she answered.

"Ah, Sujata!" cried the king, throwing aside his cloak. "Now that you have remembered what a mango is, please come back with me to my kingdom!"

Sujata fell at his feet and begged forgiveness, and the king helped her to her feet and held her tenderly. They returned together to the palace in Benares, and lived as happily as a king and queen could desire.

Regional Tales and Legends

A Demon for Work

IN A VILLAGE in South India there lived a very rich landlord who owned several villages and many fields; but he was such a great miser that he found it difficult to find tenants who would willingly work on his land, and those who did, gave him a lot of trouble. As a result, he left all his fields untilled, and even his tanks and water channels dried up. This made him poorer day by day. But he made no effort to obtain the goodwill of his tenants.

One day a holy man paid him a visit. The landlord poured out his tale of woe.

"These miserable tenants won't do a thing for me," he complained. "All my lands are going to waste."

"My dear good landlord," said the holy man, "I think I can help you, if you will repeat a *mantra* – a few magic words – which I will teach you. If you repeat it for three months, day and night, a wonderful demon will appear before you on the first day of the fourth month. He will willingly be your servant and take upon himself all the work that has been left undone by your wretched tenants. The demon will obey all your orders. You will find him equal to a hundred servants!"

The miserly landlord immediately fell at the feet of the holy man and begged for instruction. The sage gave him the magic words and then went his way. The landlord, greatly pleased, repeated the *mantra* day and night, for three months, till, on the first day of the fourth month, a magnificent young demon stood before him.

"What can I do for you, master?" he said. "I am at your command."

The landlord was taken aback by the sight of the huge monster who stood before him, and by the sound of his terrible voice, but he summoned up enough courage to say, "You can work for me provided – er – you don't expect any salary."

"Very well," said the demon, "but I have one condition. You must give me enough work to keep me busy all the time. If I have nothing to do, I shall kill you and eat you. Juicy landlords are my favourite dish."

The landlord, certain that there was enough work to keep several demons busy for ever, agreed to these terms. He took the demon to a large tank which had been dry for years, and said: "You must deepen this tank until it is as deep as the height of two palm trees."

"As you say, master," said the demon, and set to work.

The landlord went home, feeling sure that the job would take several weeks. His wife gave him a good dinner, and he was just sitting down in his courtyard to enjoy the evening breeze when the demon arrived, casually remarking that the tank was ready.

"The tank ready!" exclaimed the astonished landlord. "Why, I thought it would take you several weeks! How shall I keep him busy?" he asked, turning to his wife for aid. "If he goes on at this rate, he'll soon have an excuse for killing and eating me!"

"You must not lose heart, my husband," said the landlord's wife. "Get all the work you can out of the demon. You'll never find such a good worker again. And when you have no more work for him, let me know – I'll find something to keep him busy."

The landlord went out to inspect the tank and found that it had been completed to perfection. Then he set the demon to

78

plough all his farm lands, which extended over a number of villages. This was done in two days. He next asked the demon to dig up all the waste land. This was done in less than a day.

"I'm getting hungry," said the demon. "Come on, master, give me more work, quickly!"

The landlord felt helpless. "My dear friend," he said, "my wife says she has a little job for you. Do go and see what it is she wants done. When you have finished, you can come and eat me, because I just can't see how I can keep you busy much longer!"

The landlord's wife, who had been listening to them, now came out of the house, holding in her hands a long hair which she had just pulled out of her head.

"Well, my good demon," she said, "I have a very light job for you. I'm sure you will do it in a twinkling. Take this hair, and when you have made it perfectly straight, bring it back to me."

The demon laughed uproariously, but took the hair and went away with it.

All night he sat in a peepul tree, trying to straighten the hair. He kept rolling it against his thighs and then lifting it up to see if it had become straight. But no, it would still bend! By morning the demon was feeling very tired.

Then he remembered that goldsmiths, when straightening metal wires, would heat them over a fire. So he made a fire and placed the hair over it, and in the twinkling of an eye it frizzled and burnt up.

The demon was horrified. He dared not return to the landlord's wife. Not only had he failed to straighten the hair, but he had lost it too. Feeling that he had disgraced himself, he ran away to another part of the land.

So the landlord was rid of his demon. But he had learnt a lesson. He decided that it was better to have tenants working for him than demons, even if it meant paying for their services.

79

The Lost Ruby

ONCE UPON A TIME there lived a king, who was a great and powerful monarch. One day he was very sad, and as he sat in his council-hall surrounded by his ministers, the chief minister, who was a good and wise man, asked him: "Defender of the World! Why is your spirit sad today? Your Majesty ought not to allow grief to trouble your mind."

The king would not tell him his grief. On the contrary, he resented his good minister's concern for him. "It is all very well for you to talk," he said. "But if you had reason to be sad, I am sure you would find it impossible to practise what you have just suggested." And the king decided to put his chief minister to the test, and told him to wait at the royal palace after the council was dismissed.

The minister accordingly made his way to the royal apartments and awaited further orders. The king took out a ruby of great price from a beautiful ivory casket, and placing it in the minister's hand, told him to look after it with great care.

When the minister got home, he found his wife reclining on cushions, chewing scented *paan*. He gave her the ruby to keep. She dropped it in a partition of her cash-box and thought no more about it.

No sooner had the wily king delivered the ruby to his minister than he employed female spies to follow him up and mark where he kept the jewel. After a few days he bribed the steward of the minister's household to steal it for him. The king was sitting on the balcony of his palace overlooking the river, when the jewel was brought to him. Taking it from the hands of the steward, he deliberately threw it into the river.

The next morning, after dismissing his court, he asked the chief minister: "Where is the ruby which I gave you to keep the other day?" The minister replied: "I have got it, Defender of the World."

"Well then," said the king, "go and fetch it, for I want it right now."

Imagine the poor minister's amazement when, on going home, he understood that the ruby was nowhere to be found. He hurried back to the king and reported the loss. "Your Majesty," he said, "if you will allow me a few days grace, I hope to find it and bring it back to you."

"Very well," said the king, laughing to himself. "I give you three days in which to find the ruby. If, at the end of that time, you fail to find it, your life and the lives of all who are dear to you will be forfeit. And your house will be razed to the ground and ploughed up by donkeys!"

The minister left the palace with a heavy heart. He searched everywhere for the lost jewel, but because of its mysterious disappearance he did not have much hope of finding it.

I have no one, he thought, to whom I can leave my riches and possessions. My wife is the only soul on earth who is dear to me, and it seems we must both die after three days. What could be better than for us to enjoy ourselves during this period? We'll make the most of the time that's left to us.

In this mood he reached home and told his wife about the king's decision.

"Let us spend our wealth liberally and freely," he said, "for soon we must die."

His wife sighed deeply and only said, "As you wish. Fate has dealt us a cruel blow. Let us take it with dignity and good cheer."

That day saw the commencement of a period of great revelry in the chief minister's house. Musicians of all kinds were engaged, and the halls were filled with guests, who came wondering what great luck had come the way of the chief minister. Rich food was served, and night and day the sound of music and laughter filled the house ...

In addition, large quantities of food were prepared and given to the poor. No one who came to the house was allowed to leave empty-handed. Tradesmen, when they brought their customary presents of fresh fruit, were rewarded with gold coins, and went away rejoicing.

In a village near by there lived a poor flower-seller and a fisherwoman: the two women were neighbours and close friends. The flower-seller happened to be visiting the bazaar, where she heard of the grand doings at the minister's house. So she hurried there, with a present of vegetables and garlands, and received a gold coin. Then she walked across to her friend's house and advised her to take a present of fish to the minister, who would reward her in the same manner.

The fisherwoman was very poor. Her husband used to go fishing daily, but he seldom was able to catch large fish; those that he caught were so small that they rarely fetched more than a few pice in the bazaar. So the fisherwoman said to herself: "Those miserable fish that my husband brings home are hardly worth presenting to the minister – he'll only feel insulted", and she thought no more about it.

But the following morning, as good luck would have it, her husband caught a large Rohu, the most delicious of Indian fresh-water fish. Delighted at his good fortune, he took it home to show his wife, who immediately placed the fish in a basket, covered it with a clean cloth, and hurried to the minister's house. The minister was really pleased to see such a fine large Rohu fish, and instead of giving her one gold coin, he gave her two. The fisherwoman was overjoyed. She ran home with her prize, which was enough to keep herself and her husband in comfort for many a month.

This happened on the third and last day of the minister's life; the next day he and his wife were to be executed. Being very fond of fish-curry, he said to his wife: "Let's have one of your delightful fish-curries for lunch today. We will never be able to enjoy it again. Now here's a fine Rohu. Let's take it to the kitchen and have it cleaned."

He and his wife sat together to see the fish cut. The cook took out his kitchen-knife and set to work.

As the cook thrust his knife into the fish's belly, out dropped the ruby which had been thrown into the river.

The minister and his wife were overcome with astonishment and joy. They washed the ruby in perfumed water, and then the minister hastened to restore it to the king.

The king was equally amazed to see the ruby which he had thrown into the river. He at once demanded an explanation for its recovery. The minister told him how he had decided to spend all his riches, and how he had received the present of a fish which, when it was cut, gave up the lost ruby.

The king then acknowledged the part he had played in the loss of the ruby, "But I see that you took your own advice to me," he said. "Endure sorrow cheerfully!" He bestowed high honours on his minister, and commended his wisdom and understanding before all his courtiers and ministers.

And so the minister's evil fortune was changed to good.

"And may the Eternal Dispenser of all Good thus deal with his servants".

How a Tribal Boy
Became a King

ONCE UPON A TIME there was a Bhuiya tribal boy, who was left an orphan when he was very young. The villagers used to give him food, and when he grew up, he was sent to graze cattle in the jungle. At night he used to sleep on a small platform which he had set up in a banyan tree.

God Indra pitied the youth and sent a fairy from his heavenly court with a tray of the finest food. But the young man was afraid to look at her, and, whenever she came, he would close his eyes in terror.

After some days he told an old woman of the tribe about the fairy's visits. The old woman said: "This food is sent by Lord Indra. If you don't eat it, he will be displeased. But if you do not want the fairy to visit you, the next time she comes, just cut off a piece of the cloth which covers her breast."

When the fairy came again the next night and asked the Bhuiya to eat, he pulled out the curved knife which he used to peel bamboos, and cut off a piece of her dress. After that she stopped visiting him.

One day the village people said to their barber: "It is time that young man's head was shaved."

So the barber went to where the Bhuiya was staying in the jungle.

In those days a barber was reputed to be the craftiest of men. There was even a proverb which went: "As the crow is among birds, so is the barber among men." As the barber was shaving the youth's head, he saw the piece from the fairy's robe, and thought: "Such fine cloth is not found even in a king's palace."

"Where did you get this?" he asked.

"My uncle gave it to me," answered the youth.

The barber went to the king and told him about the lovely piece of cloth he had seen with the Bhuiya. The king sent for the youth and said, "You must get me a bale of this cloth."

"I will get it if you give me three hundred rupees," said the Bhuiya.

The king gave him the money, and with it the youth bought a horse for two hundred rupees, and the rest he spent on good clothes. Then he rode off in search of the cloth.

Presently he came to the outskirts of a city, and halted at a water tank to bathe and water his horse. Some soldiers of the chief of that city saw him, and one of them said: "This must be some great prince. Our chief has a daughter for whom he cannot find a suitable husband. If he were to marry her to this prince, his troubles would be over."

So they told the chief about the handsome prince who was mounted on a fine horse, and he sent for the youth.

"Who are you?" he asked.

"I am a chief's son," said the Bhuiya.

"If another king offered you his daughter in marriage, would you accept her?"

"I would have to obtain the consent of my parents and brothers."

"If you refuse to marry her, I will have you killed."

"In that case I must marry her," said the Bhuiya.

So they were married the next day, with much feasting and ceremony.

"I have some urgent business at home," said the young man

afterwards," but I will return in a few days and take my wife home."

So the Bhuiya youth rode off, and after some hard riding he reached the palace of a powerful queen, Balwanti Rani, who lived in the depths of a thick jungle. The palace had seven gates, one within the other. The first was guarded by a demon, whose upper lip stretched to heaven and lower lip to Patala, the underworld. When the Bhuiya saw him, he thought, This monster's mouth will engulf me and my horse. I had better make friends with him. Better still, I will claim a relationship.

So he went up to the demon and said: "I salute you, O maternal Uncle!"

The demon said: "I have had no food for twelve years, and when prey comes my way, it is hard that it should turn out to be my sister's son. All the same, sit down and tell me what you want."

"I am here to enquire about the health of Balwanti Rani," said the youth.

"Do not ask about her," said the demon. "She sleeps for twelve years and remains awake for twelve years. Just now she is asleep, and as a result all her guards and servants are dying of hunger."

"How can I manage to see her, Uncle?"

"It's very difficult. She has seven guards. The first is myself. Next comes a tiger guard; then a leopard guard; then a bear guard. Then come guards of demons and witches. You cannot see the Rani unless you get past all these guards."

"Well, I must see her, and as my uncle you must tell me how to evade the guards."

"Very well," said the demon. "Take he-goats for the tiger and the leopard. Take some wild plums for the bear. And take some parched rice for the demons and witches. They are very hungry, and if you feed them, they may let you in. But be careful on your return, as they will then attack you."

The Bhuiya took these presents with him, and did as he was told, and no one paid any attention to him. Then he entered a chamber where Balwanti Rani lay asleep on a couch of gold. Under her bed was a betel box, containing the ingredients for making *paan*. The boy took some *paan*, chewed it, and with the red spittle he made a mark on the cloth which covered her breast. Then he went away.

As he returned, all the guards rushed at him, but he threw rice before the demons and witches, goats before the tiger and leopard, and a handful of wild plums before the bear. And so he escaped to where his adopted uncle was on guard. He mounted the horse, and, saluting his demon-uncle, rode away.

Next day Balwanti Rani finally woke up, and prepared for her bath. But when she saw the red mark on her robe she was very angry. She was determined to find the person who had dared to mark her robe. She mounted on her flying couch, and after many days reached the tank where the Bhuiya had met the soldiers of the king. There he was, bathing and watering his horse.

"Why did you run away after marking my robe?" demanded Balwanti Rani. "Now I must live with you all my life!" And they were married on the spot.

That night, while her husband slept, Balwanti Rani built a palace much grander than that of any king. Next morning the Bhuiya saw the palace and told Balwanti Rani to stay there while he went to see the father of his first wife. The chief received him kindly, and that night the youth stayed with his first wife, the chief's daughter.

When they were alone together, the girl said, "If my father asks you to accept a present, take nothing but the basket in

which cowdung is collected for the palace. It has magic powers, and all my father's prosperity depends on it."

Next day the chief offered many valuable presents to his son-in-law, but the young man said: "I will have nothing but the cowdung basket."

The chief was very upset. "Take anything but that worthless basket."

But the Bhuiya would have nothing except the basket, and at last the chief had to give it to him, and he took it and his wife to the palace which Balwanti Rani had built. Then they all returned to the Bhuiya's native village, and that night his two wives built a palace even more splendid than the last.

A few days later the old barber arrived. When he shaved the Bhuiya's head, he recognised him. Then he went and pared the nails of the two wives. After this he went back to the king and said: "The Bhuiya to whom you gave money to buy cloth has come back rolling in wealth, and he has two beautiful wives who are fit only for a king."

"How do I get hold of them?" asked the king.

"Send for the youth," said the barber, "and demand your cloth. He won't be able to produce it, and will have to give you the women instead."

The king sent for the Bhuiya and asked, "Where is the cloth you promised to bring me?"

"You shall have it tomorrow," said the Bhuiya.

When he got home, Balwanti Rani saw that he was worried and asked him the reason. He told her how he was in the king's power.

"Don't worry," she said. "I am the fairy whose breast-cloth you cut. I will bring you four bales of the cloth tomorrow."

Next day the Bhuiya gave the cloth to the amazed king.

Then the barber said: "Tell him to bring you four baskets of ripe mangoes. They are out of season, and he is sure to fail. Then he will have to give up his women."

Again the Bhuiya youth was troubled, until Balwanti Rani solved the problem, for by her magical powers she planted a garden that night, and in the morning the trees were laden with ripe mangoes. These the youth gave to the king.

"Our plans have failed again," said the barber. "But let us try another trick. Call the Bhuiya and tell him to bring you news of your parents in the world of the dead."

When the king gave this order, the Bhuiya was very worried. But when Balwanti Rani heard the story, she said: "Go to the king and say that, in order that you may be able to visit the land of the dead, you must have a house filled with fuel. In this you must be burnt so that your spirit can go to Yama."

While the preparations were being made, Balwanti Rani made an underground passage from this place to her own house, and when the fire was lit, the Bhuiya escaped by the passage to his home. He stayed indoors for six months, living in the dark, letting his hair and beard grow. Then he came out and said to the king, "Yamaraj is a terrible place. Look at my condition after being there for six months. Just think of what your parents must be, who have been there twelve years!"

The king was determined to go and see his parents for himself. He had a house filled with fuel and lighted. Then he stepped into the fire and went up in flames. And the Bhuiya took possession of the kingdom, and ruled it for many years with justice and wisdom.

The Happy Herdsman

A YOUNG HERDSMAN was watching some sheep at the edge of the jungle, when a tiger came out and asked him for a sheep.

"They are not my sheep," said the herdsman. "How can I give you one?"

"All right, don't," said the tiger. "I'll eat you instead, one of these nights."

When the herdsman came home, he told his mother what had happened, and she said, "We had better get the neighbours to sleep in the house, as a precaution."

So the neighbours brought their beds and slept in the house. The herdsman's bed was placed in the centre. In the middle of the night the tiger came in quietly, crept under the herdsman's bed, and carried it off on his shoulders.

When they had gone a little distance, the herdsman fortunately woke, to find himself being borne away on his bed. As they passed under a huge banyan tree, he caught hold of one of its dangling shoots and climbed up. The tiger, knowing nothing of this, went off with the bed.

The herdsman was so afraid of the tiger that he remained in the tree all next day. In the evening a herd of cows came to the spot and lay down under the banyan tree. They remained there all night and next morning went off to graze. While they were away, the herdsman came down and cleaned up the area under the banyan tree.

Next night, when the cows came again, they were delighted to find that someone had cleaned the area. They wondered who had done them this service. When the same thing happened three days in succession, the cows called out, "Show yourself, oh unknown friend! We are grateful, and wish to make your acquaintance." But the herdsman thought this might be some trick on the part of the tiger. He kept quiet and remained hidden in the banyan tree.

Then the cows made a plan. One of them was old and weak, so the others told her: "You lie here and pretend to be sick. Our friend is sure to come down to help you after we have gone. When he comes, catch hold of his *dhoti*, and don't let go until we return."

The old cow did as she was told. When she caught hold of the herdsman's *dhoti*, he did his best to drag himself away, but she held fast.

When the cows came back, they told the herdsman how grateful they were to him. They said, "You may have as much of our milk as you want."

So the herdsman continued to live in the banyan tree, and he would milk the cows every day.

One day, as he was walking about beneath the tree, he saw several young snakes coming out of a hole in the ground. They looked thin and miserable. The herdsman felt sorry for them, so every day he gave them some milk. When they grew strong and began to move about in the jungle, they met their mother, who exclaimed: "I can't believe it! I left you starving, and now here you are, well and strong!" They told her how the herdsman had taken care of them. So she went to the herdsman and said: "Ask any boon you will." And the herdsman said: "I wish that my hair and skin would turn the colour of gold." The change took place almost at once, and then the snakes went away.

On a hot summer's day the herdsman went down to the river to bathe. As he was bathing, a strand of golden hair came away in his hands. He made a little leaf-boat, and he put the hair in it, and let it float downstream.

Many miles downstream a king's daughter was bathing. As the leaf-boat floated past, she picked up the golden hair. "Oh, how lovely!" she exclaimed. "My father must marry me to the man who has hair like this!"

When she showed her father the hair, and told him of her desire to marry its owner, the king made every effort to find him. Finally his soldiers traced the herdsman and told him to accompany them back to the king's palace. "I will do nothing of the sort," he said.

They tried to drag him away, but he played on his flute and all the cows rushed up, charged the soldiers and drove them off.

When they told the king what had happened, he sent his pet crows to get the flute. They came and perched on the banyan tree, and made a lot of noise. The herdsman threw stones at them, but could not drive them away. Finally he became so angry that he threw his flute at them. One of the crows caught it neatly in its beak and flew off with it.

Having got possession of the flute, the king sent another party of soldiers to seize the herdsman. He blew upon another flute, but this one did not have the same magic, and the cows did not rush to his rescue. He was carried off to the king's palace.

The king lost no time in marrying the herdsman to the princess. They were given a beautiful house and lots of money. But, although the herdsman was fond of his wife, he longed for his former life as a cowherd.

One day he asked his wife to give him the old flute. She took it out of her box and gave it to him. When he blew it, the sound reached the cows, and they all rushed to the king's palace and began knocking down the walls.

The king was terrified and asked them what they wanted.

"We want our cowherd!" they replied.

So the king had to give in. But, being a king, he built a palace for his son-in-law near the banyan tree, and gave him half his kingdom. The palace remained empty, because the herdsman and his princess preferred to stay in the banyan tree, where they lived happily together for many a year.

The Tiger-King's Gift

L ONG AGO in the days of the ancient Pandya kings of South India, a father and his two sons lived in a village near Madura. The father was an astrologer, but he had never become famous, and so was very poor. The elder son was called Chellan; the younger Gangan. When the time came for the father to put off his earthly body, he gave his few fields to Chellan, and a palm leaf with some words scratched on it to Gangan.

These were the words that Gangan read:

> *"From birth, poverty;*
> *For ten years, captivity;*
> *On the seashore, death.*
> *For a little while happiness shall follow."*

"This must be my fortune," said Gangan to himself, "and it doesn't seem to be much of a fortune. I must have done something terrible in a former birth. But I will go as a pilgrim to Papanasam and do penance. If I can expiate my sin, I may have better luck."

His only possession was a water jar of hammered copper, which had belonged to his grandfather. He coiled a rope round the jar, in case he needed to draw water from a well. Then he put a little rice into a bundle, said farewell to his brother, and set out.

As he journeyed he had to pass through a great forest. Soon he had eaten all his food and drunk all the water in his jar. In the heat of the day he became very thirsty.

At last he came to an old, disused well. As he looked down into it he could see that a winding stairway had once gone round it down to the water's edge, and that there had been four landing places at different heights down this stairway; so that those who wanted to fetch water might descend the stairway to the level of the water and fill their water-pots with ease, regardless of whether the well was full, or three-quarters full, or half full or only one quarter full.

Now the well was nearly empty. The stairway had fallen away. Gangan could not go down to fill his water-jar so he uncoiled his rope, tied his jar to it and slowly let it down. To his amazement, as it was going down past the first landing place, a huge striped paw shot out and caught it, and a growling voice called out: "Oh Lord of Charity, have mercy! The stair is fallen. I die unless you save me! Fear me not. Though King of Tigers, I will not harm you."

Gangan was terrified at hearing a tiger speak; but his kindness overcame his fear, and with a great effort, he pulled the beast up.

The Tiger King – for it was indeed the Lord of All Tigers – bowed his head before Gangan, and reverently paced round him thrice from right to left as worshippers do round a shrine.

"Three days ago," said the Tiger King, "a goldsmith passed by, and I followed him. In terror he jumped down this well and fell on the fourth landing place below. He is there still. When I leaped after him I fell on the first landing place. On the third landing is a rat who jumped in when a great snake chased him. And on the second landing, above the rat, is the snake who followed him. They will all clamour for you to draw them up.

"Free the snake, by all means. He will be grateful and will not harm you. Free the rat, if you will. But do not free the goldsmith,

for he cannot be trusted. Should you free him, you will surely repent of your kindness. He will do you an injury for his own profit. But remember that I will help you whenever you need me."

Then the Tiger King bounded away into the forest.

Gangan had forgotten his thirst while he stood before the Tiger King. Now he felt it more than before, and again let down his water-jar.

As it passed the second landing place on the ruined staircase, a huge snake darted out and twisted itself round the rope. "Oh, Incarnation of Mercy, save me!" it hissed. "Unless you help me, I must die here, for I cannot climb the sides of the well. Help me, and I will always serve you!"

Gangan's heart was again touched, and he drew up the snake. It glided round him as if he were a holy being. "I am the Serpent King," it said. "I was chasing a rat. It jumped into the well and fell on the third landing below. I followed, but fell on the second landing. Then the goldsmith leaped in and fell on the fourth landing place, while the tiger fell on the top landing. You saved the Tiger King. You have saved me. You may save the rat, if you wish. But do not free the goldsmith. He is not to be trusted. He will harm you if you help him. But I will not forget you, and will come to your aid if you call upon me."

Then the King of Snakes disappeared into the long grass of the forest.

Gangan let down his jar once more, eager to quench his thirst. But as the jar passed the third landing, the rat leaped into it.

"After the Tiger King, what is a rat?" said Gangan to himself, and pulled the jar up.

Like the tiger and the snake, the rat did reverence, and offered his services if ever they were needed. And like the tiger and the snake, he warned Gangan against the goldsmith. Then the Rat King – for he was none other – ran off into a hole among the roots of a banyan tree.

By this time Gangan's thirst was becoming unbearable. He almost flung the water-jar down the well. But again the rope was seized, and Gangan heard the goldsmith beg piteously to be hauled up.

"Unless I pull him out of the well, I shall never get any water," groaned Gangan. "And after all, why not help the unfortunate man?" So with a great struggle – for he was a very fat goldsmith – Gangan got him out of the well and on to the grass beside him.

The goldsmith had much to say. But before listening to him, Gangan let his jar down into the well a fifth time. And then he drank till he was satisfied.

"Friend and deliverer!" cried the goldsmith. "Don't believe what those beasts have said about me! I live in the holy city of Tenkasi, only a day's journey north of Papanasam. Come and visit me whenever you are there. I will show you that I am not an ungrateful man." And he took leave of Gangan and went his way.

"From birth, poverty."

Gangan resumed his pilgrimage, begging his way to Papanasam. There he stayed many weeks, performing all the ceremonies which pilgrims should perform, bathing at the waterfall, and watching the Brahmin priests feeding the fishes in the sacred stream. He visited other shrines, going as far as Cape Comorin, the southernmost tip of India, where he bathed in the sea. Then he came back through the jungles of Travancore.

He had started on his pilgrimage with his copper water-jar and nothing more. After months of wanderings, it was still the only thing he owned. The first prophecy on the palm leaf had already come true: "From birth, poverty."

During his wanderings Gangan had never once thought of the Tiger King and the others, but as he walked wearily along in his rags, he saw a ruined well by the roadside, and it reminded him of his wonderful adventure. And just to see if the Tiger King was genuine, he called out: "Oh King of Tigers, let me see you!"

No sooner had he spoken than the Tiger King leaped out of the bushes, carrying in his mouth a glittering golden helmet, embedded with precious stones.

It was the helmet of King Pandya, the monarch of the land.

The king had been waylaid and killed by robbers, for the sake of the jewelled helmet; but they in turn had fallen prey to the tiger, who had walked away with the helmet.

Gangan of course knew nothing about all this, and when the Tiger King laid the helmet at his feet, he stood stupefied at its splendour and his own good luck.

After the Tiger King had left him, Gangan thought of the goldsmith. "He will take the jewels out of the helmet, and I will sell some of them. Others I will take home." So he wrapped the helmet in a rag and made his way to Tenkasi.

In the Tenkasi bazaar he soon found the goldsmith's shop. When they had talked awhile, Gangan uncovered the golden helmet. The goldsmith – who knew its worth far better than Gangan – gloated over it, and at once agreed to take out the jewels and sell a few so that Gangan might have some money to spend.

"Now let me examine this helmet at leisure," said the goldsmith. "You go to the shrines, worship, and come back. I will then tell you what your treasure is worth."

Gangan went off to worship at the famous shrines of Tenkasi. And as soon as he had gone, the goldsmith went off to the local magistrate.

"Did not the herald of King Pandya's son come here only yesterday and announce that he would give half his kingdom to anyone who discovered his father's murderer?" he asked. "Well, I have found the killer. He has brought the king's jewelled helmet to me this very day."

The magistrate called his guards, and they all hurried to the goldsmith's shop and reached it just as Gangan returned from his tour of the temples.

"Here is the helmet!" exclaimed the goldsmith to the magistrate. "And here is the villain who murdered the king to get it!"

The guards seized poor Gangan and marched him off to Madura, the capital of the Pandya kingdom, and brought him before the murdered king's son. When Gangan tried to explain about the Tiger King, the goldsmith called him a liar, and the new king had him thrown into the death-cell, a deep, well-like pit, dug into the ground in a courtyard of the palace. The only entrance to it was a hole in the pavement of the courtyard. Here Gangan was left to die of hunger and thirst.

At first Gangan lay helpless where he had fallen. Then, looking around him, he found himself on a heap of bones, the bones of those who before him had died in the dungeon; and he was watched by an army of rats who were waiting to gnaw his dead body. He remembered how the Tiger King had warned him against the goldsmith, and had promised help if ever it was needed.

"I need help now," groaned Gangan, and shouted for the Tiger King, the Snake King, and the Rat King.

For some time nothing happened. Then all the rats in the dungeon suddenly left him and began burrowing in a corner between some of the stones in the wall. Presently Gangan saw that the hole was quite large, and that many other rats were

102

coming and going, working at the same tunnel. And then the Rat King himself came through the little passage, and he was followed by the Snake King, while a great roar from outside told Gangan that the Tiger King was there.

"We cannot get you out of this place," said the Snake King. "The walls are too strong. But the armies of the Rat King will bring rice-cakes from the palace kitchens, and sweets from the shops in the bazaars, and rags soaked in water. They will not let you die. And from this day on the tigers and the snakes will slay tenfold, and the rats will destroy grain and cloth as never before. Before long the people will begin to complain. Then, when you hear anyone passing in front of your cell, shout: 'These disasters are the results of your ruler's injustice! But I can save you from them!' At first they will pay no attention. But after some time they will take you out, and at your word we will stop the sacking and the slaughter. And then they will honour you."

"For ten years, captivity."

For ten years the tigers killed. The serpents struck. The rats destroyed. And at last the people wailed, "The gods are plaguing us."

All the while Gangan cried out to those who came near his cell, declaring that he could save them; they thought he was a madman. So ten years passed, and the second prophecy on the palm leaf was fulfilled.

At last the Snake King made his way into the palace and bit the king's only daughter. She was dead in a few minutes.

The king called for all the snake-charmers and offered half his kingdom to any one of them who would restore his daughter to life. None of them was able to do so. Then the king's servants remembered the cries of Gangan and remarked that there was a madman in the dungeons who kept insisting that he could bring an end to all their troubles. The king at once ordered the dungeon to be opened. Ladders were let down. Men descended and found Gangan, looking more like a ghost than a man. His hair had grown so long that none could see his face. The king did not remember him, but Gangan soon reminded the king of how he had condemned him without enquiry, on the word of the goldsmith.

The king grovelled in the dust before Gangan, begged forgiveness, and entreated him to restore the dead princess to life.

"Bring me the body of the princess," said Gangan.

Then he called on the Tiger King and the Snake King to come and give life to the princess. As soon as they entered the royal chamber, the princess was restored to life.

Glad as they were to see the princess alive, the king and his courtiers were filled with fear at the sight of the Tiger King and the Snake King. But the tiger and the snake hurt no one; and at a second prayer from Gangan, they brought life to all those they had slain.

And when Gangan made a third petition, the Tiger, the Snake and the Rat Kings ordered their subjects to stop pillaging the Pandya kingdom, so long as the king did no further injustice.

"Let us find that treacherous goldsmith and put him in the dungeon," said the Tiger King.

But Gangan wanted no vengeance. That very day he set out for his village to see his brother, Chellan, once more. But when he left the Pandya king's capital, he took the wrong road. After much wandering, he found himself on the sea-shore.

Now it happened that his brother was also making a journey in those parts, and it was their fate that they should meet by the sea. When Gangan saw his brother, his gladness was so sudden and so great that he fell down dead.

And so the third prophecy was fulfilled:

"On the sea-shore, death."

Chellan, as he came along the shore road, had seen a half-ruined shrine of Pillaiyar, the elephant-headed God of Good Luck. Chellan was a very devout servant of Pillaiyar, and, the day being a festival day, he felt it was his duty to worship the god. But it was also his duty to perform the funeral rites for his brother.

The sea-shore was lonely. There was no one to help him. It would take hours to collect fuel and driftwood enough for a funeral pyre. For a while Chellan did not know what to do. But at last he took up the body and carried it to Pillaiyar's temple.

Then he addressed the god. "This is my brother's body," he said. "I am unclean because I have touched it. I must go and bathe in the sea. Then I will come and worship you, and afterwards I will burn my brother's body. Meanwhile, I leave it in your care."

Chellan left, and the god told his attendant *Ganas* (goblins) to watch over the body. These *Ganas* are inclined to be mischievous, and when the god wasn't looking, they gobbled up the body of Gangan.

When Chellan came back from bathing, he reverently worshipped Pillaiyar. He then looked for his brother's body. It was not to be found. Anxiously he demanded it of the god. Pillaiyar called on his goblins to produce it. Terrified, they confessed to what they had done.

Chellan reproached the god for the misdeeds of his attendants. And Pillaiyar felt so much pity for him, that by his divine power he restored dead Gangan's body to Chellan, and brought Gangan to life again.

The two brothers then returned to King Pandya's capital, where Gangan married the princess and became king when her father died.

And so the fourth prophecy was fulfilled:

> *"For a little while happiness shall follow."*

But there are wise men who say that the lines of the prophecy were wrongly read and understood, and that the whole should run:

> *"From birth, poverty;*
> *For ten years, captivity;*
> *On the sea-shore, death for a little while;*
> *Happiness shall follow."*

It is the last two lines that are different. And this must be the correct version, because when happiness came to Gangan it was not "for a little while." When the Goddess of Good Fortune did arrive, she stayed in his palace for many, many years.

The Ghost and the Idiot

IN A VILLAGE near Agra there lived a family who was under the special protection of a *Munjia*, a ghost who lived in a peepul tree. The ghost had attached himself to this particular family and showed his fondness for its members by throwing stones, bones, night-soil and other rubbish at them, and making hideous noises, terrifying them at every opportunity. Under his patronage, the family dwindled away. One by one they died, the only survivor being an idiot boy, whom the ghost did not bother because he felt it beneath his dignity to do so.

But in an Indian village, marriage (like birth and death) must come to all, and it was not long before the neighbours began to make plans for the marriage of the idiot.

After a meeting of the village elders it was decided, first, that the idiot should be married; and second, that he should be married to a shrew of a girl who had passed the age of twenty without finding a suitor!

The shrew and the idiot were soon married off, then left to manage for themselves. The poor idiot had no means of earning a living and had to resort to begging. He had barely been able to support himself before, and now his wife was an additional burden. The first thing she did when she entered the house was to give him a box on the ear and send him out to bring something home for dinner.

The poor fellow went from door to door, but nobody gave

him anything, because the same people who had arranged the marriage were annoyed that he had not given them a wedding feast. In the evening, when he returned home empty-handed, his wife cried out: "Are you back, you lazy idiot? Why have you been so long, and what have you brought for me?"

When she found he hadn't even a paisa, she flew into a rage and, removing his head-cloth, tossed it into the peepul tree. Then, taking up her broom, she belaboured her husband until he fled from the house.

But the shrew's anger had not yet been assuaged. Seeing her husband's head-cloth in the peepul tree, she began venting her rage on the tree-trunk, accompanying her blows with the most shocking abuse. The ghost who lived in the tree was sensitive to both her blows and her language. Alarmed that her terrible curses might put an end to him, he took to his heels and left the tree in which he had lived for so many years.

Riding on a whirlwind, the ghost soon caught up with the idiot who was still fleeing down the road away from the village.

"Not so fast, brother!" cried the ghost. "Desert your wife, by all means, but don't abandon your old family ghost! That shrew has driven me out of the peepul tree. What powerful arms she has – and what a vile tongue! She has made brothers of us – brothers in misfortune. And so we must seek our fortunes together! But first promise me you will not return to your wife."

The idiot made this promise very willingly, and together they journeyed until they reached a large city.

Before they entered the city, the ghost said, "Now listen, brother. If you follow my advice, your fortune is made. In this city there are two very beautiful girls, one the daughter of a king and the other the daughter of a rich money-lender. I will go and possess the daughter of the king, and when he finds her possessed by a spirit he will try every sort of remedy but with no effect. Meanwhile you must walk daily through the streets in the dress of a *Sadhu* – one who has renounced the world – and when the king comes and asks you if you can cure his daughter, undertake to do so and make your own terms. As soon as I see you, I shall leave the girl. Then I shall go and possess the daughter of the money-lender. But do not go near her, because I am in love with the girl and do not intend giving her up! If you come near her, I shall break your neck."

The ghost went off on his whirlwind, while the idiot entered the city on his own and found a bed at the local inn for pilgrims.

The following day everyone in the city was agog with the news that the king's daughter was dangerously ill. Physicians of all sorts came and went, and all pronounced the girl incurable. The king was on the verge of a nervous breakdown. He offered half his fortune to anyone who could cure his beautiful and only child. The idiot, having smeared himself with dust and ashes like a *Sadhu*, began walking the streets, reciting religious verses.

The people were struck by the idiot's appearance. They took him for a wise and holy man, and reported him to the king, who immediately came into the city, prostrated himself before the idiot, and begged him to cure his daughter. After a show of modesty and reluctance, the idiot was persuaded to accompany the king back to the palace, and the girl was brought before him.

Her hair was dishevelled, her teeth were chattering, and her eyes almost starting from their sockets. She howled and cursed and tore at her clothes. The idiot confronted her and recited a few meaningless spells. And the ghost, recognising him, cried out in terror: "I'm going, I'm going! I'm on my way!"

"Give me a sign that you have gone," demanded the idiot.

"As soon as I leave the girl," said the ghost, "you will see that mango tree uprooted. That is the sign I'll give."

A few minutes later the mango tree came crashing down. The

girl recovered from her fit and seemed unaware of what had happened. The news of her miraculous cure spread through the city, and the idiot became an object of veneration and wonder. The king kept his word and gave him half his fortune; and so began a period of happiness and prosperity for the idiot.

A few weeks later the ghost took possession of the money-lender's daughter, with whom he was in love. Seeing his daughter take leave of her senses, the money-lender sent for the highly respected idiot and offered him a great sum of money to cure his daughter. But remembering the ghost's warning, the idiot refused. The money-lender was enraged and sent his henchmen to bring the idiot to him by force; and the idiot was dragged along to the rich man's house.

As soon as the ghost saw his old companion, he cried out in a rage: "Idiot, why have you broken our agreement and come here? Now I will have to break your neck!"

But the idiot, whose reputation for wisdom had actually helped to make his wiser, said, "Brother ghost I have not come to trouble you but to tell you a terrible piece of news. Old friend and protector, we must leave this city soon. SHE has come here – my dreaded wife! – to torment us both, and to drag us back to the village. She is on her way and will be here any minute!"

When the ghost heard this, he cried out, "Oh no, oh no! If SHE has come, then we must go!"

And breaking down the walls and doors of the house, the ghost gathered himself up into a little whirlwind and went scurrying out of the city to look for a vacant peepul tree.

The money-lender, delighted that his daughter had been freed of the evil influence, embraced the idiot and showered presents on him. And in due course the idiot married the money-lender's beautiful daughter, inherited his wealth and debtors, and became the richest and most successful money-lender in the city.

Brave and Beautiful

ONCE UPON A TIME there ruled a Rajput king called Kesarising. He had a daughter, Sunderbai, who was her father's chief treasure: not only was she well versed in the arts and sciences, but she was brave and generous; and as for her beauty, she had no equal among the princesses of India.

In spite of her learning, Sunderbai was as light-hearted as any of her friends and companions. One day she was playing with other girls in the palace gardens, when the crown prince of Valabhipura, Birsing, happened to pass by. He had been out hunting; and now, hot and tired, he lay down to rest beneath some trees in the garden. While he was resting, he heard voices close by. At first he paid no attention. But as the voices grew louder, he could not help overhearing.

"When I marry," said one of the girls, "I shall lead my husband a life of it! Men trample on their wives just as if they were pieces of furniture. And yet, if a man has no wife, he is quite useless."

"You are quite right," answered Sunderbai. "But I am going to marry Prince Birsing, the son of the king of Valabhipura. And I mean so to win his love that he will have eyes for no other. If he does not treat me as I mean him to, I shall show him by my strength and courage that women are every bit as brave as men. He will so love and honour me that he will never take a second wife."

Birsing was all attention when he heard his name. He realised that the second speaker must be the king's daughter. He decided to slip away before he was seen; but before he went, he looked through the trees at Sunderbai. He was quite taken by her beauty; but he looked thoughtful as he rode away.

When the prince reached his own home, he told the king, his father, that he wanted to marry Kesarising's daughter. As the two families were equal in rank, there was no obstacle in the way. And before long, the wedding was celebrated with great splendour, and Sunderbai was carried in state to Birsing's palace.

The young prince wished to see whether Sunderbai would make good her boast. And so, on their marriage night, he did not go near her. The princess wondered at his conduct, and her maid-servants and companions wondered still more. But Sunderbai hid her feelings.

Months passed, and then one of the princess's maids came and said to her, "Princess, today is New Year's day, and there is a great festival at the temple. Would you not like to go and see it?" Sunderbai agreed, and at once prepared to go.

Early in the morning she left her palace, and went with her maids and ladies to the temple. When Birsing heard that Sunderbai had gone to the temple, he also went there with some of his courtiers, unseen by her. As she worshipped, she prayed aloud, "Goddess Parvati, bless in all ways my husband!" Then she raised her head, and, as she did so, her eyes met those of Birsing, who had come up quietly behind her.

He gave her a mocking smile, and said, "Is this the way you mean to conquer your husband – by strength and valour, as you boasted once?"

Sunderbai then knew that Birsing had overheard her that day in the garden. Clasping her hands, she answered, "Lord, women are but foolish creatures. A girl's chatter should not be taken seriously. Pay no heed to what was said, and in your wisdom forgive me."

But Birsing shook his head and answered sternly, "Until you make good your words, princess, I will not enter the door of your palace." And he turned away and left the temple.

Sunderbai stood looking after him, the picture of distress. Then, deciding that if she wanted to win him, she would have to give him proof of her courage and strength, she finished her worship and left the temple.

Sunderbai spent several days pondering what she should do. At last she resolved to leave the palace. The Goddess Parvati might send her the chance which she sought. But to leave the palace and slip through the guards was no easy thing. So she took from her finger a ring, given her by her father, Kesarising; and handing it to one of her trusted companions, she said, "Take this to the king, my father, and say, 'The jewel in the ring is loose. Please have it put right.'"

The girl did as she was asked, and when Kesarising saw the ring, he guessed that his daughter was in trouble. After the messenger had gone, he took out the stone. Beneath it was a note, on which was written: My father, when two parrots quarrel, it is useless to keep them in the same cage. One day in the garden I told one of my companions that if I married Birsing, I would by my strength and valour make him madly in love with me. The prince overheard what I said, and is putting me to the test. Send me a man's dress, a coat of mail, and a swift horse. But let no one know.

The king managed to send the horse, clothes, and armour to his daughter by means of a secret passage into her palace. Sunderbai donned the dress and the coat of mail, and warned her maids and companions to tell no one of her flight. Then,

mounting her horse, she rode away in the dead of night.

Two days later a bold and handsome youth came to Valab-hipura, and asked to see the king. When the king asked the stranger his name and that of his father, the youth replied: "My name is Ratan Singh. My father is a Rajput, but I have quarrelled with him, and I have come to you in search of service. Any work you give me, I will do."

The king liked the bold and fearless bearing of the young Rajput and at once gave him a place among his nobles. Ratan Singh soon proved his mettle. By his skill in riding he always out-distanced the other nobles. Birsing became very fond of him; and, never suspecting his identity, told him in the strictest confidence all about Sunderbai's pride and arrogance, and how he had taught her a lesson. Ratan Singh laughed and said, "You are not treating her very kindly, are you?" To which Birsing replied, "I really love her more than anyone else in the world; nor will I every marry anyone else. But I want to test her and see if she will make good her boast. If she is a true Rajputni, she will do so."

Not long afterwards a fierce lion began to haunt the outskirts of Valabhipura. Every day it killed and ate one or two of the inhabitants. The young nobles did their best to destroy it, but none succeeded. Then Ratan Singh decided to hunt the man-eater.

First he asked the king's craftsmen to make him a hollow iron image of a man. Then he had the image placed in a spot where the lion had killed several men, got inside it, and sent away the men who had brought it. At midnight the lion came, and, taking the image to be a man, rushed at it. As the lion tried in vain to knock the image over, Ratan Singh slipped out, and with a single blow of his sword severed the lion's head.

When the king heard about this heroic feat, he bestowed on Ratan Singh a robe of honour and a grant of land.

A few months later the king was hunting in a distant forest, accompanied by Ratan Singh. A neighbouring king heard through his spies of the king's absence, and, making a surprise attack, took Valabhipura. Birsing had been ill and had not gone with his father to the hunt: he too fell into the enemy's hands. Having captured the capital and the heir-apparent, the neighbouring king set up strong defences round the city.

When the news reached the king he was broken-hearted. "Oh my son Birsing," he cried in Ratan Singh's hearing. "If they kill you, how can I live?"

Ratan Singh did his best to comfort the old king, then rode swiftly to his father's kingdom and told Kesarising all that had happened. Taking with him a picked body of lancers, he returned to the old king's camp. There he divided his men into four squadrons of fifty each. He had three of them attack different parts of the city, while he himself entered the city through the secret passage, took the garrison by surprise, and, after overcoming the enemy, opened the gates for the other squadrons. They soon recaptured the city. Ratan Singh then freed Birsing from the dungeon in which he had been imprisoned, and, after embracing him, took him to his father.

A little later Ratan Singh excused himself, saying that he had to see some friends who had just come from his old home. When he did not return, Birsing began to look for him. But he could find him not. At last some men told him that they had seen Ratan Singh enter Sunderbai's palace.

A dark suspicion entered Birsing's mind.

"Ratan Singh," he said to himself, "must be my wife's lover. That is how he learnt about the secret entrance. Through it he must have gone to have secret meetings with her."

Drawing his sword, he rushed up the steps that led to Sunderbai's chamber. She was alone, and rose to greet him; but her humility only added fuel to his anger.

"Where is your Ratan Singh, you faithless woman?" he cried.

Sunderbai, amazed at the question, answered, "Of whom do you speak, Lord?"

Birsing grew even more furious. "You wretch!" he cried. "You know well of whom I speak. Where is Ratan Singh, your lover, who came to you by the secret passage into your palace? Show me where he is hidden, that I may cut off his head, and then stab you to the heart!"

Sunderbai drew herself to her full height and said, "What better death could I wish than death at your hands? But before you stab me, look well into my face. Perhaps you may find there your friend Ratan Singh, with whom you are now so angry."

Birsing looked into Sunderbai's face. She smiled at him mockingly. At once he recognised her as Ratan Singh, who had saved his father's throne and his own life. He fell at her feet and implored her pardon.

"Confess, my lord," said Sunderbai teasingly, "that I have redeemed the pledge I made in my father's garden, and that women can be every bit as brave as men."

"They can be as brave as they are beautiful," said Birsing, and embraced her tenderly.

Seven Brides for
Seven Princes

A LONG TIME AGO there was a king who had seven
sons – all of them brave, handsome and clever. The old king
loved them equally, and the princes dressed alike and received
the same amounts of pocket money. When they grew up they
were given separate palaces, but the palaces were built and
furnished alike, and if you had seen one palace you had seen the
others.

When the princes were old enough to marry, the king sent his
ambassadors all over the country to search out seven brides of
equal beauty and talent. The ambassadors travelled everywhere
and saw many princesses but could not find seven equally
suitable brides. They returned to the king and reported their
failure.

The king now became so despondent and gloomy that his
chief minister decided that something had to be done to solve his
master's problem.

"Do not be so downcast, Your Majesty," he said. "Surely it is
impossible to find seven brides as accomplished as your seven
sons. Let us trust to chance, and then perhaps we shall find the
ideal brides."

The minister had thought out a scheme, and when the princes
agreed to it, they were taken to the highest tower of the fort,
which overlooked the entire city as well as the surrounding
countryside. Seven bows and seven arrows were placed before

them, and they were told to shoot in any direction they liked. Each prince had agreed to marry the girl upon whose house the arrow fell, be she daughter of prince or peasant.

The seven princes took up their bows and shot their arrows in different directions, and all the arrows except that of the youngest prince fell on the houses of well-known and highly-respected families. But the arrow shot by the youngest brother went beyond the city and out of sight.

Servants ran in all directions looking for the arrow and, after a long search, found it embedded in the trunk of a great banyan tree, in which sat a monkey.

Great was the dismay and consternation of the king when he discovered that his youngest son's arrow had made such an unfortunate descent. The king and his courtiers and his minister held a hurried conference. They decided that the youngest prince should be given another chance with his arrow. But to everyone's surprise, the prince refused a second chance.

"No," he said. "My brothers have found beautiful and good brides, and that is their good fortune. But do not ask me to break the pledge I took before shooting my arrow. I know I cannot marry this monkey. But I will not marry anyone else! Instead I shall take the monkey home and keep her as a pet."

The six lucky princes were married with great pomp. The city was ablaze with lights and fireworks, and there was music and dancing in the streets. People decorated their houses with the leaves of mango and banana trees. There was great rejoicing everywhere, except in the palace of the youngest prince. He had placed a diamond collar about the neck of his monkey and seated her on a chair cushioned with velvet. They both looked rather melancholy.

"Poor monkey," said the prince. "You are as lonely as I am

on this day of rejoicing. But I shall make your stay here a happy one! Are you hungry?" And he placed a bowl of grapes before her, and persuaded her to eat a few. He began talking to the monkey and spending all his time with her. Some called him foolish, or obstinate; others said he wasn't quite right in the head.

The king was worried and discussed the situation with his minister and his other sons, in a bid to find some way of bringing the prince to his senses and marrying him into a noble family. But he refused to listen to their advice and entreaties.

As the months passed, the prince grew even more attached to his monkey, and could be seen walking with her in the gardens of his palace.

Then one day the king called a meeting of all seven princes and said, "My sons, I have seen you all settled happily in life. Even you, my youngest, appear to be happy with your strange companion. The happiness of a father consists in the happiness of his sons and daughters. Therefore I wish to visit my daughters-in-law and give them presents."

The eldest son immediately invited his father to dine at his palace, and the others did the same. The king accepted all their invitations, including that of the youngest prince. The receptions were very grand, and the king presented his daughters-in-law with precious jewels and costly dresses. Eventually it was the turn of the youngest son to entertain the king.

The youngest prince was very troubled. How could he invite his father to a house in which he lived with a monkey? He knew his monkey was more gentle and affectionate than some of the greatest ladies in the land; and he was determined not to hide her away as though she were someone to be ashamed of.

Walking beside his pet in the palace gardens, he said, "What shall I do now, my friend? I wish you had a tongue with which to

comfort me. All my brothers have shown their homes and wives to my father. They will ridicule me when I present you to him."

The monkey had always been a silent and sympathetic listener when the prince spoke to her. Now he noticed that she was gesturing to him with her hands. Bending over her, he saw that she held a piece of broken pottery in her hand. The prince took the shard from her and saw that something was written on it. These were the words he read:

"Do not worry, sweet prince, but go to the place where you found me, and throw this piece of pottery into the hollow trunk of the banyan tree, and wait for a reply."

The prince did as he was told. Going to the ancient banyan tree, he threw the shard of pottery into the hollow, and then stood back to see if anything would happen.

He did not have to wait long.

A beautiful fairy dressed in green stepped out of the hollow, and asked the prince to follow her. She told him that the queen of the fairies wished to see him in person.

The prince climbed the tree, entered the hollow, and after groping about in the dark was suddenly led into a spacious and wonderful garden, at the end of which stood a beautiful palace. Between an avenue of trees flowed a crystal-clear stream, and on the bed of the stream, instead of pebbles, there were rubies and diamonds and sapphires. Even the light which lit up this new world was warmer and less harsh than the light of the world outside. The prince was led past a fountain of silver water, up steps of gold, and in through the mother-of-pearl doors of the palace. But the splendour of the room into which he was led seemed to fade before the exquisite beauty of the fairy princess who stood before him.

"Yes, prince, I know your message," said the princess. "Do not be anxious, but go home and prepare to receive your father the king and your royal guests tomorrow evening. My servants will see to everything."

Next morning, when the prince awoke in his palace, an amazing sight met his eyes. The palace grounds teemed with life. The gardens were full of pomegranate trees, laden with fruit, and under the trees were gaily decorated stalls serving sweets, scented-water and cooling sherbets. Children were playing on the lawns, and men and women were dancing or listening to music.

The prince was bewildered by what he saw, and he was even more amazed when he entered his banquet hall and found it full of activity. Tables groaned under the weight of delicious pillaus, curries and biryanis. Great chandeliers hung from the ceiling, bunches of roses filled the room with their perfume.

A servant came running to announce that the king and his courtiers were arriving. The prince hurried out to meet them. After dinner was served, everyone insisted on seeing the companion the prince had chosen for himself. They thought the monkey would make excellent entertainment after such a magnificent feast.

The prince could not refuse this request, and passed gloomily through his rooms in search of his monkey. He feared the ridicule that would follow. This, he knew, was his father's way of trying to cure him of his obstinacy.

He opened the door of his room and was almost blinded by a blaze of light. There, on a throne in the middle of the room, sat the fairy princess.

"Come, prince," she said. "I have sent away the monkey and I am here to offer you my hand."

On hearing that his pet had gone, the prince burst into tears. "What have you done?" he cried. "It was cruel of you to take away my monkey. Your beauty will not compensate me for the loss of my companion."

"If my beauty does not move you," said the princess with a smile, "let gratitude help you take my hand. See what pains I have taken to prepare this feast for your father and brothers. As my husband, you shall have all the riches and pleasures of the world at your command."

The prince was indignant. "I did not ask these things of you – nor do I know what plot has been afoot to deprive me of my monkey. Restore her to me, and I will be your slave!"

Then the fairy princess came down from her throne, and taking the prince by the hand, spoke to him with great love and respect.

"You see in me your friend and companion," she said. "Yes, it was I who took the form of a monkey, to test your faith and sincerity. See, my monkey's skin lies there in the corner."

The prince looked, and saw in a corner of the room the skin of his monkey.

He joined the fairy princess on her throne, and when she said "Arise, arise, arise," the throne rose in the air and floated into the hall where the guests had gathered.

The prince presented his bride to his father, who was of course delighted. The guests were a little disappointed to find that their hostess was not, after all, a monkey. But they had to admit that the prince and the princess made a most handsome couple.

A Battle of Wits

IN A VILLAGE in northern India there lived a Bania,
a merchant whose shop kept the villagers supplied with their
everyday necessities.

One day, on his way to a neighbouring town to make some
purchases, he met a poor Jat, one of a tribe of farmers who was
also going to town to pay the monthly instalment of a debt he
owed to the local *mahajan*, the banker and moneylender.

The debt had actually been incurred by the Jat's great-
grandfather and had in the beginning been only fifty rupees; but
his great grandfather had been unable to repay it, and in the last
fifty years, through interest and compound interest, the amount
had grown to five hundred rupees.

The Jat was walking along, wondering if he would ever get out
of the clutches of the *mahajan*, when the Bania caught up with
him.

"Good day to you, Chowdhri," said the Bania, who, though
he had a poor opinion of the farmer's intelligence, was always
polite to his customers. "I see you are going to town to pay your
instalment to the *mahajan*. Before long you will have to give up
your lands. Can nothing be done to save them?"

"It is too late to do anything, Shahji," said the Jat. He was
much taller and stronger than the Bania; at the same time he was
an easy-going, good-natured sort. The Bania thought he was
simple-minded.

"Well, let us forget our worries," said the Bania, "and pass the time telling stories."

"A good idea, Shahji! It will make the journey less tiresome. But let there be one condition. No matter how fantastic or silly the story, neither of us must call it untrue. Whoever does so, must pay the other five hundred rupees!"

"Agreed," said the Bania with a laugh. "And let me begin my story first. My great-grandfather was the greatest of Banias, and tremendously rich."

"True, oh Shahji, true!" said the Jat.

"At one time he possessed a fleet of forty ships with which he sailed to China, and traded there in rich jewels and costly silks."

"True, oh Shahji, true!" said the Jat.

"Well, after making a huge fortune my great-grandfather returned home with many unique and precious things. One was a statue of pure gold which was able to answer any question put to it."

"True, oh Shahji, true!"

"When my great-grandfather came home, many people came to have their questions answered by his wonderful statue. One day *your* great-grandfather came with a question. He asked: 'Who are the wisest of all men?' The statue replied: 'The Banias, of course.' Then he asked: 'And who are the most foolish?' The statue replied: 'The Jats.' And then your great-grandfather asked, 'Among the Jats, who is the most stupid?' The statue replied: 'Why, you are, of course.'"

"True, oh Shahji, true," said the Jat, inwardly resolving to repay the Bania in his own coin.

"My father," continued the Bania, "was himself a great traveller, and during a tour of the world he saw many wonders. One day, a mosquito hovering near his ear threatened to bite him. My father, not wishing to kill the mosquito, requested it to

126

leave. The mosquito was amazed at such gentlemanly conduct. It said, 'Noble Shahji, you are the greatest man I ever met, and I mean to do you a great service.' Saying this, the mosquito opened its mouth, and inside it my father saw a large palace with golden doors and windows. At one of the windows stood the most beautiful princess in the world. At the door of the palace he saw a peasant about to attack the princess. My father, who was very brave, at once jumped into the mouth of the mosquito and entered its stomach. He found it very dark inside."

"True, oh Shahji, true!" said the Jat.

"Well, after some time my father grew used to the darkness and was able to make out the palace, the princess and the peasant. He at once fell upon the peasant, who happened to be *your* father. They fought for a year in the stomach of the mosquito. At the end of that time your father was defeated and became my father's servant. My father then married the princess and I was born from the union. But when I was fifteen years old, a heavy rain of boiling water fell on the palace, which collapsed, throwing us into a scalding sea. With great difficulty we swam ashore, where the four of us found ourselves in a kitchen, where a woman was shaking with terror at the sight of us."

"True, oh Shahji, true!"

"When the woman, who was a cook, realized that we were men and not ghosts, she complained that we had spoilt her soup. 'Why did you have to enter my pot of boiling water and frighten me like that?' she complained. We apologised, explaining that for fifteen years we had been living in the belly of a mosquito, and that it was not our fault that we had found ourselves in her cooking pot. 'Ah! I remember now,' she said. 'A little while ago a mosquito bit me on the arm. You must have been injected into my arm, for when I squeezed out the poison, a large black drop fell into the boiling water. I had no idea you were in it!'"

"True, oh Shahji, true!" said the Jat.

"Well, when we left the kitchen we found ourselves in another country, which happened to be our present village. Here we took to shopkeeping. The princess, my mother, died many years ago. That, Chowdhri, is my story. Improve upon it if you can!"

"A very true story," said the Jat. "My story, though no less true, is perhaps not as wonderful. But it is perfectly true, every word of it...

"My great-grandfather was the wealthiest Jat in the village. His noble appearance and great wisdom brought praise from all who met him. At village meetings he was always given the best seat, and when he settled disputes no one questioned his good judgement. In addition, he was of great physical strength, and a terror to the wicked."

"True, oh Chowdhri, true," said the Bania.

"There was a time when a great famine came to our village. There was no rain, the rivers and wells dried up, the trees withered away. Birds and beasts died in thousands. When my great-grandfather saw that the village stores had been exhausted, and that the people would die of hunger if something was not done, he called the Jats together and said, 'Brother Jats, God Indra is angry with us for some reason, because he has withheld the seasonal rains. But if you do what I tell you, I will supply you all with food until the scarcity is over. I want you to give your fields to me for six months.' Without any hesitation the Jats gave my great-grandfather their fields. Then, stripping himself of his clothes, he gave one great heave and lifted the entire village of a thousand acres and placed it on his head!"

"True, oh Chowdhri, true!" exclaimed the Bania.

"Then my great-grandfather, carrying the village on his head, searched for rain...

"Wherever there was rain he took the village, so that the

rainwater fell on the fields and collected in the wells. Then he told the Jats (who were of course still in the village on his head) to plough their land and sow their seed. The crops that came up had never been so wonderful, and the wheat and the maize rose to such a height that they touched the clouds."

"True, oh Chowdhri, true," said the Bania.

"Then my great-grandfather returned to his country and placed the village in its proper place. The farmers reaped a record harvest that year. Ever grain of corn was as big as your head."

"True, oh Chowdhri, true," said the Bania, annoyed at the comparison but anxious not to lose his wager. By this time, they had reached the outskirts of the town, but the Jat had not finished his story.

"At that time *your* great-grandfather was a very poor man," said the Jat, "and mine, who had made huge profits from his wonderful harvest, employed him as a servant to weigh out the grain for the customers."

"True, oh Chowdhri, true," said the Bania with a sour look.

"Being a blockhead, your ancestor often made mistakes for which he would receive thrashings from my great-grandfather."

"True, oh Chowdhri, true!"

By this time they had entered the shop of the *mahajan* to whom the Jat was owing money. Bidding the banker good morning, they sat down on the floor in front of him. But the Jat, without speaking to the banker, continued his story.

"Well, Shahji, after my great-grandfather sold his harvest he discharged your great-grandfather. But, before he went, your ancestor asked mine for a loan of fifty rupees, which was generously given to him."

"True, oh Chowdhri, true!" said the Bania.

"Very good," said the Jat, raising his voice so that the

mahajan could also hear them. "Your ancestor did not repay that debt. Nor did your grandfather, or your father, repay the debt. Neither have you repaid it up to this time."

"True, oh Chowdhri, true!"

"Now that sum of fifty rupees, with interest and compound interest, amounts to exactly five hundred rupees, which sum you owe me!"

"True, oh Chowdhri, true!"

"So, as you have admitted the debt before the *mahajan*, kindly pay the amount to him so that I may have my lands released."

This placed the Bania in a dilemma. He had admitted a debt before a third party. If he said that it was merely a story, and completely untrue, he would have to pay the Jat five hundred rupees according to the terms of the wager. If he said it was true, he would have to pay the amount to the *mahajan*. Either way he was the loser.

So the Bania paid up, and never again did he belittle the intelligence of his Jat neighbours.

Toria and the
Daughter of the Sun

ONCE UPON A TIME there was a young shepherd of the Santal tribe named Toria, who grazed his sheep and goats on the bank of a river. Now it happened that the daughters of the Sun would descend from heaven every day by means of a spider's web, to bathe in the river. Finding Toria there, they invited him to bathe with them. After they had bathed and anointed themselves with oils and perfumes, they returned to their heavenly abode, while Toria went to look after his flock.

Having become friendly with the daughters of the Sun, Toria gradually fell in love with one of them. But he was at a loss to know how to obtain such a divine creature. One day, when they met him and said, "Come along, Toria, and bathe with us," he suddenly thought of a plan.

While they were bathing, he said, "Let us see who can stay under water the longest." At a given signal they all dived, but very soon Toria raised his head above water and, making sure that no one was looking, hurried out of the water, picked up the robe of the girl he loved, and was in the act of carrying it away when the others raised their heads above the water.

The girl ran after him, begging him to return her garment, but Toria did not stop till he had reached his home. When she arrived, he gave her the robe without a word. Seeing such a beautiful and noble creature before him, for very bashfulness he could not open his mouth to ask her to marry him; so he simply said, "You can go now."

But she replied, "No, I will not return. My sisters by this time will have gone home. I will stay with you, and be your wife."

All the time this was going on, a parrot, whom Toria had taught to speak, kept on flying about the heavens, calling out to the Sun: "Oh, great Father, do not look downwards!" As a result, the Sun did not see what was happening on earth to his daughter.

This girl was very different from the women of the country – she was half human, half divine – so that when a beggar came to the house and saw her, his eyes were dazzled just as if he had stared at the Sun.

It happened that this same beggar in the course of his wanderings came to the king's palace, and having seen the queen, who was thought by all to be the most beautiful of women, he told the king: "The shepherd Toria's wife is far more beautiful than your queen. If you were to see her, you would be enchanted."

"How can I see her?" asked the king eagerly.

The beggar answered, "Put on your old clothes and travel in disguise."

The king did so, and having arrived at the shepherd's house, asked for alms. Toria's wife came out of the house and gave him food and water, but he was so astonished at seeing her great beauty that he was unable to eat or drink. His only thought was, How can I manage to make her my queen?

When he got home he thought over many plans and at length decided upon one. He said, "I will order Toria to dig a large tank with his own hands, and fill it with water, and if he does not perform the task, I will kill him and seize his wife." He then summoned Toria to the palace, commanded him to dig the tank and threatened him with death if he failed to fill the tank with water the same night.

Toria returned home slowly and sorrowfully.

"What makes you so sad today?" asked his wife.

He replied, "The king has ordered me to dig a large tank, to fill it with water, and also to make trees grow beside it, all in the course of one night."

"Don't let it worry you," said his wife. "Take your spade and mix a little water with the sand, where the tank is to be, and it will form there by itself."

Toria did as he was told, and the king was astonished to find the tank completed in time. He had no excuse for killing Toria.

Later, the king planted a great plain with mustard seed. When it was ready for reaping, he commanded Toria to reap and gather the produce into one large heap on a certain day; failing which, he would certainly be put to death.

Toria, hearing this, was again very sad. When he told his wife about it, she said, "Do not worry, it will be done." So the daughter of the Sun summoned her children, the doves. They came in large numbers, and in the space of an hour carried the produce away to the king's threshing-floor. Again, Toria was saved through the wisdom of his wife. However, the king determined not to be outdone, so he arranged a great hunt. On the day of the hunt he assembled his retainers, and a large number of beaters and provision-carriers, and set out for the jungle. Toria was employed to carry eggs and water. But the object of the hunt was not to kill a tiger, it was to kill Toria, so that the king might seize the daughter of the Sun and make her his wife.

Arriving at a cave, they said that a hare had taken refuge in it. They forced Toria into the cave. Then, rolling large stones against the entrance, they completely blocked it. They gathered large quantities of brushwood at the mouth of the cave, and set fire to it to smother Toria. Having done this, they returned home, boasting that they had finally disposed of the shepherd. But Toria broke the eggs, and all the ashes were scattered. Then he poured the water that he had with him on the remaining embers, and the fire was extinguished. Toria managed to crawl out of the cave. And there, to his great astonishment, he saw that all the white ashes of the fire were becoming cows, whilst the half-burnt wood was turning into buffaloes.

Toria herded the cows and buffaloes together, and drove them home.

When the king saw the herd, he became very envious, and asked Toria where he had found such fine cows and buffaloes. Toria said, "From that cave into which you pushed me. I did not bring many with me, being on my own. But if you and all your retainers go, you will be able to get as many as you want. But to catch them it will be necessary to close the door of the cave, and light a fire in front, as you did for me."

"Very well," said the king. "I and my people will enter the cave, and, as you have sufficient cows and buffaloes, kindly do not go into the cave with us, but kindle the fire outside."

The king and his people then entered the cave. Toria blocked up the doorway, and then lit a large fire at the entrance. Before long, all that were in the cave were suffocated.

Some days later the daughter of the Sun said, "I want to visit my father's house."

Toria said, "Very well, I will also go with you."

"No, it is foolish of you to think of such a thing," she said. "You will not be able to get there."

"If you are able to go, surely I can." And he insisted on accompanying her.

After travelling a great distance, Toria became so faint from the heat of the sun that he could go no further. His wife said,

"Did I not warn you? As for quenching your thirst, there is no water to be found here. But sit down and rest, I will see if I can find some for you."

While she was away, driven by his great thirst, Toria sucked a raw egg that he had brought with him. No sooner had he done this than he changed into a fowl. When his wife returned with water, she could not find him anywhere; but, sitting where she had left him, was a solitary fowl. Taking the bird in her arms, she continued her journey.

When she reached her father's house, her sisters asked her, "Where is Toria, your husband?" She replied, "I don't know. I left him on the road while I went to fetch water. When I returned, he had disappeared. Perhaps he will turn up later."

Her sisters, seeing the fowl, thought that it would make a good meal. And so, while Toria's wife was resting, they killed and ate the fowl. Later, when they again enquired of her as to the whereabouts of her husband, she looked thoughtful.

"I can't be sure," she said. "But I think you have eaten him."

The Wicked Guru

A CERTAIN KING of the South had a beautiful daughter. When she had reached a marriageable age, the king spoke to his Guru (spiritual teacher) and said: "Tell me, O Guru, by the stars the auspicious day for my daughter's marriage."

But the Guru had become enamoured of the girl's beauty, and he answered with guile, "It will be wrong to celebrate your daughter's marriage at this time. It will bring evil on both of you. Instead, adorn her with thirty-six ornaments and clothe her in the finest of her garments, cover her with flowers and sprinkle her with perfumes, and then set her in a spacious box afloat on the waters of the ocean."

It was the time of Dwapara Yuga – the third age of the world – and the Guru had to be obeyed. So they did as he said, to the great sorrow of the king and all his subjects. The king asked the Guru to stay and comfort them, but he said he had to return at once to his sacred seat, and left for his own home some three days distant.

As soon as he reached his house, the Guru stocked it with gold and pearl and silver and coral and the finest of fabrics that women delight in, and called his three hundred and sixty disciples and said: "My children, go and search the ocean, and whoever finds floating on it a large box, bring it here, and do not come to me again until I summon you."

They all scattered to do as they had been told.

Meanwhile, the king of a neighbouring country had gone hunting on the sea-shore, where he had wounded a bear in the leg. The wounded bear limped about and gave vent to short savage grunts. As the king looked out to sea, he saw a box floating on the crests of the waves. He was quite a young man, and, being an expert swimmer, he soon brought the box ashore. Great was his surprise and joy to find that it contained a beautiful girl adorned as a bride.

He put the lame bear into the box and set it afloat once again. Then he hurried home with his prize. The girl was only too glad to marry her deliverer, and a great wedding took place.

All this time the Guru's disciples were searching for the box, and when one of them found it floating near the shore he duly brought it to the Guru, and then disappeared as he had been told. The Guru was delighted. He prepared sweets and fruits and flowers and scents. He closed all the doors of his chamber. He could hardly contain himself as he opened the box.

As soon as the box was open, out jumped the bear, savage and hungry and at war with all human-beings because of the treatment he had received. He seized the Guru in a bear-hug and then tore out his throat.

Feeling his life ebbing, the Guru dipped his finger in his own blood and wrote this *Sloka*:

> *Man's desires are not fulfilled.*
> *The God's desires prevail.*
> *The king's daughter is in the king's palace.*
> *The bear has eaten the priest.*

When the Guru failed to send for his disciples, they went together to his house, where, on breaking open his chamber-door, they found his body. The Guru's murder appeared to be a mystery, until the king, who had been sent for, found the verses

on the wall and had them translated by his scholars. One scholar proved that the bear could have escaped by means of a large drain that was found in the building.

Now it happened that this king was related to the neighbouring king who had found and married the princess in the box, and went to visit him.

"How remarkably like my daughter," he remarked, on seeing his hostess.

"Yes, the same daughter who was set afloat in a box," said the queen. But they were overjoyed to see each other again; and the king was especially pleased, because he had all along hoped that his daughter would marry the king-next-door.

"As Your Liberality,
So Your Virtue"

A BRAHMIN who had no children used to go every day to the king's palace, and say, "As your liberality, so your virtue."

He did this daily for a year and six months, and received a rupee each time.

At last the king began to wonder why he was bothering to give away a rupee every day, so he asked the Brahmin, "What do you mean by the saying, 'As your liberality, so your virtue', which you keep repeating every day?"

The Brahmin had no idea – it was just a phrase he had been taught to repeat since childhood – so he went home and thought about it, but the king gave him nothing that day; and what was worse, the king said that if the Brahmin failed to come up with a suitable explanation, he would sacrifice him before the Goddess Durga.

That very day a daughter was born to the childless Brahmin, and as soon as she came from the womb, she smiled, stood up, and said, "Father, why do you look so sad?"

The father replied, "What is the use of telling you? You were only born today." But his baby daughter again said, "Father, let me hear about it. Why is your face so sad?"

So her father answered, "Every day since I was a boy, I have been going to the king's palace and saying, 'As your liberality, so your virtue.' Every time I received a rupee. But today the king has threatened to sacrifice me to the Goddess Durga if I do not explain the *meaning* of the saying to him. Now isn't that unreasonable? Why should anyone want to know the meaning of something that has been accepted as the truth for centuries?"

His daughter told him to go and bathe, and said she would give him the meaning of the saying. So he went and bathed; and, after he had eaten, he returned to his daughter. She told him to go to the court, and if the king spoke to him, to say, "Your majesty, two days ago a daughter was born in my house. She will tell you the meaning of the saying."

The father did just as he was told. The king was astonished, and declared that it was nonsense to suppose that an infant could explain the meaning of anything. Nevertheless, he took his elephants, horses and soldiers, and went to the Brahmin's house.

When the little girl saw the king, she stood up and asked him why he had come to her home. When he told her, she said, "I can tell you the meaning of the saying, but for the moment I will only say this: in the southern corner of your kingdom lives an oil-man, and his red ox will tell you."

So the king took away his elephants, horses and soldiers, and went to the oil-man's house, and asked him whether he kept a red ox to turn his oil mill.

"There he is in the field," said the oil-man.

The king went up to the ox and said, "Ho, Mr. Oil-man's ox, can you tell me the meaning of the saying, 'As your liberality, so your virtue'?"

The ox replied weeping, "I would tell you if I could, but I will only say that there is a clump of Sheora trees to the east of your palace, and they will tell you."

So the king took his elephants, horses and soldiers, and went to the clump of Sheora trees and said, "Good Sheora trees, tell me the meaning of the saying, 'As your liberality, so your virtue'."

The genius of the Sheora trees replied: "Listen, king of the world, you have been made a king because in your former life you were very kind and liberal, and gave your whole mind to charity. The woman who was then your wife was very pure in heart, and she has now been born in the house of the childless Brahmin. The oil-man's red ox was formerly your son. And now, last of all, I must explain that I was once your son's wife, but my heart was hardened against everyone, and I was most unwilling to give anything away; so in the end I became the spirit, or genius, of this grove of trees. I cannot move from here. Our destinies are controlled by the actions of our former lives."

On hearing this the king returned home. Every day after that the Brahmin went to the palace, and repeated the saying, and received his rupee.

The Song of
the Whistling-Thrush

IN THE WOODED HILLS of western India lives "The Idle Schoolboy" – a bird who cannot learn a simple tune though he is gifted with one of the most beautiful voices in the forest. He whistles away in various sharps and flats, and sometimes, when you think he is really going to produce a melody, he breaks off in the middle of his song as though he had just remembered something very important.

Why is it that the Whistling-Thrush can never remember a tune? The story goes that on a hot summer's afternoon the young God Krishna was wandering along the banks of a mountain stream when he came to a small waterfall, shot through with sunbeams. It was a lovely spot, cool and inviting. Tiny fish flecked the pool at the foot of the waterfall, and a Paradise Flycatcher, trailing its silver tail, moved gracefully amongst the trees.

Krishna was enchanted. He threw himself down on a bed of moss and ferns, and began playing on his flute – the famous flute with which he had charmed all the creatures in the forest. A fat yellow lizard nodded its head in time to the music; the birds were hushed; and the shy mouse-deer approached silently on their tiny hooves to see who it was who played so beautifully.

Presently the flute slipped from Krishna's fingers, and the beautiful young god fell asleep. But it was not a restful sleep, for his dreams were punctuated by an annoying whistling, as though someone who didn't know much about music was practising on his flute in an attempt to learn the tune that Krishna had been playing.

Awake now, Krishna sat up and saw a ragged urchin standing ankle-deep in the pool, the sacred flute held to his lips!

Krishna was furious.

"Come here, boy!" he shouted. "How dare you steal my flute and disturb my sleep! Don't you know who I am?"

The boy, instead of being afraid, was thrilled at the discovery that he stood before his hero, the young Krishna, whose exploits were famous throughout the land.

"I did not steal your flute, lord," he said. "Had that been my intention, I would not have waited for you to wake up. It was only my great love for your music that made me touch your flute. You will teach me to play, will you not? I will be your disciple."

Krishna's anger melted away, and he was filled with compassion for the boy. But it was too late to do anything, for it is everlastingly decreed that anyone who touches the sacred property of the gods, whether deliberately or in innocence, must be made to suffer throughout his next ten thousand births.

When this was explained to the boy, he fell on his face and wept bitterly, crying, "Have mercy on me, Krishna. Do with me as you will, but do not send me away from the beautiful forests I love."

Swiftly, Krishna communed in spirit with Brahma the Creator. Here was a genuine case of a crime committed in ignorance. If it could not be forgiven, surely the punishment could be less severe?

Brahma agreed, and Krishna laid his hand on the boy's mouth, saying, "For ever try to copy the song of the gods, but never succeed." Then he touched the boy's clothes and said, "Let the raggedness and dust disappear, and only the beautiful colours of

Krishna remain."

Immediately the boy was changed into the bird we know today as the Whistling Thrush of Malabar, with its dark body and brilliant blue patches on head and wings. In this guise he still continues to live among the beautiful, forested valleys of the hills, where he tries unsuccessfully to remember the tune that brought about his strange transformation.

Notes and Sources

TALES FROM THE EPICS
LOVE CONQUERS ALL

The story of Savitri is found in the *Mahabharata*, the great epic poem of India, which contains much of the mythology and religion of the Hindus. It is divided into eighteen books and contains about 220,000 lines, which must make it the longest poem in the world. Over the centuries (500 B.C.–400 A.D.) the poem received many additions. It tells the epic story of the great wars between the two branches of the Bharata family (the Pandavas and the Kauravas). The date of the war itself was probably in the 14th century B.C. The tale of Savitri is told to the exiled King of the Pandavas to console him for the plight of his enslaved Queen Draupadi. The story of Savitri has been used as the basis for a short opera by Gustav Holst, composed in 1907.

THE COW OF PLENTY

This is how the story ends in the *Mahabharata*. But the *Ramayana*, the other great Hindu epic, tells us that, before admitting defeat, Vishwamitra made another violent attempt to overcome the power of Vasishtha. It describes a great slaughter on both sides, and says that it took a mighty effort on the part of the cow before she gained the final victory.

Many of the sacred hymns of the *Rig-Veda* (see note on *The Superior Man*) are attributed to Vasishtha. He was considered one of the seven great sages of the ancient world.

In India the cow is reverenced as "the fountain of milk and curds."

KING BHARATA

Tales of Bharata, an ancient king, are well-known in south India, and appear in early Telegu literature – the *Telegu Vaishnavas* – and also in the *Vishnu*

147

Puranas, sacred Hindu texts written in approximately 400 A.D.

This is not the same Bharata, half brother of Rama, whose story is told in the *Ramayana*; nor is he the son of Dushyanta and Shakuntala.

Kali: The goddess Kali is terrible to look upon. She has four, sometimes ten, arms, and in her hands are deadly weapons ... Kali or Kalika means "the black", and she is represented with a black skin, dripping blood, encircled with snakes, and hung round with skulls and human heads... The female energy of the God Shiva has two aspects, one mild, the other fierce, and Kali represents one form of the latter.

Brahmin: A Brahmin belongs to the priestly order, the highest caste in the system of Hinduism. The sacred thread (worn over the left shoulder and extending half-way down the right thigh) is first worn when a Brahmin boy is about eight years old; the thread must be made by a Brahmin priest. A Brahmin youth cannot be married before he has received the thread.

SHIVA'S ANGER

This story is found both in the *Ramayana* and the *Mahabharata*. Although these epic poems contain many accounts, like this one, of the might and majesty of the gods, they also deal with the actions of mortals and their romantic adventures as in the story of Savitri.

Daksha: One of the ten great Rishis, or Sages, "mind-born sons of Brahma", from whom mankind has descended. *Shiva*, the great God, is known as the Destroyer and Reproducer. His wife is known by several names and in several characters, and here she is Uma, "light and beautiful", the mountain goddess.

In concluding this tale, the *Mahabharata* goes on to say: "If you read this story and recite the names of Shiva you will never be troubled by fever, and more than that, you will never experience the slightest evil all through life."

NALA AND DAMAYANTI

The story is told as an episode in the *Mahabharata*. It first became known in England by being translated into English verse by Dean Milman. According to one scholar (Balfour), "Being a domestic story, it is better fitted than battles to the Hindu genius, and is a model of beautiful simplicity."

The *Mahabaharata* goes on to tell us that Nala and Damayanti lived happily together for some time, a son and daughter being born to them. But

Notes and Sources

Nala was lured on to gamble with Pushkara, who used charmed dice. Nala lost kingdom, wife and children, and he wandered off a pauper. After various fortunes, he and Damayanti met again and were reunited. He had learned how to play with dice, and challenged Pushkara, from whom he recovered all he had lost.

Swayamvara: From the Sanskrit, *Swayam*, herself; and *Vara*, choosing – indicating that the lady did indeed choose for herself.

THE SUPERIOR MAN

Vedas: The sacred hymns of the Vedic period, begun as early as 1500 B.C. The *Rig-Veda* is the oldest, and to a large extent the source from which the later collections of hymns are drawn. It is essentially a book of praise addressed to the nature gods of the Aryans. 'Veda' means 'divine knowledge'. This story is found in the *Mahabharata* (500 B.C.).

SHAKUNTALA

Bharata: Has given his name to India (Bharata-varsha). The wars of his descendants are described in the *Mahabharata*. Even though this story has its origins in the *Mahabharata*, *Shakuntala* is probably best-known as a verse-play written by Kalidas, India's greatest poet-dramatist, who lived in the 4th century A.D. It was the first translation made from Sanskrit into English (by Sir William Jones, in the late 18th century). After *Shakuntala*, the best-known of Kalidas's plays is the *Mrichikata*, or *Toy Cart*. See also: *The Lost Ruby*.

TALES FROM THE JATAKA
THE HARE IN THE MOON

When English children look up at the moon, they see marked on it the figure of a man with a bundle of sticks, and by his side a dog. To the eyes of Indian children the dog seems more like a hare. In Sanskrit the moon is called *sasin*, "having a hare". This story is found in the *Jataka*, the great collection of Buddhist birth-stories, in which the Bodhisattva (Buddha) visits the earth in various forms – in this case as a hare. Many of the stories in the *Jataka* are, in fact, adaptations of even earlier Indian tales. In the *Kalmuk* (Central Asian) version of the legend, it is the soul of the hare that is transferred to the moon. The God Sakka (not found in Hindu mythology) appears in many of the Jataka tales, where he is described as "King of the Gods".

THE UGLY PRINCE AND THE HEARTLESS PRINCESS

This is one of the several stories in the *Jataka* which is not a beast fable. The legends in the *Jataka* relate to Sakya Muni, or Buddha's previous existences, which he is said to have related at various times to his hearers, and in which much of his teaching is to be found. In this story, God Sakka decides the Buddha should go again into the world of men, where he is born as Prince Kusa.

Sitar: A stringed instrument.

THE CRANE AND THE CRAB

This is one of the best known beast fables in the *Jataka*, the Buddhist Birth-stories, which draw upon even earlier stores of Indian folklore. The Buddha used this tale to draw the following moral:

> "The villain, though exceeding clever,
> Shall prosper not by his villainy.
> He may win, indeed, sharp-witted in deceit,
> But only as the crane here from the crab."

(In the Birth-story, the Buddha has been looking on at the drama in the form of a tree-spirit).

This tale is an excellent example of how the world's folklore is inter-related. It is found in the Arabic *Kalila-wa-Damna*, the Persian *Anwar-i-Suhaili*, The Greek *Stephanites kai Ichnelates*, the French *Livres des Lumières* and *Cabinet des Fées*, in La Fontaine, the Arabian Nights, the Indian *Panchatantra* and *Hitopadesa*, and many other collections of house-hold stories. In the *Panchatantra* (composed about 200 B.C.), the crab crawls back to his old pond, dragging the crane's head with him, as a warning to the remaining inhabitants of the pond.

FRIENDS IN DEED

In this tale from the *Jataka*, which extols the virtues of true friendship, the Buddha assumes the form of the Antelope. The three friends, we are told, lived long and happily and then "passed away to be rewarded according to their deeds".

150

Notes and Sources

"WHO'LL BUY MY MANGOES?"

I have adapted this story from a short tale in the *Jataka*. King Brahmadatta reigns at Benares, and the Buddha (in the guise of a minister) persuades the king to forgive his wife.

Benares (Varanasi): Also called Kashi by the Hindus, has been the religious capital of India from beyond historical times. It is mentioned in both the *Mahabharata* and *Ramayana*. Six centuries before the Christian era, the Buddha came to Benares to establish his religion.

REGIONAL TALES AND LEGENDS
A DEMON FOR WORK

This tale from south India first appeared in the English rendering by Pandit S. M. Natesa Sastri, in *The Indian Antiquary*, Vol. XVI, October 1887. The story explains the custom of nailing a handful of hair to a tree in which evil spirits are supposed to dwell, in order to drive them away.

THE LOST RUBY

"May the Eternal Dispenser of all Good thus deal with his servants" – that's how an Indian tale was traditionally made to end by its narrator. This was a popular folk-tale in northern India during the 19th century, when the Moghul kings still ruled at Delhi.

Persian was the court language of the Moslem rulers, and the Persian influence on Indian literature was quite marked during the Moghul period (1525–1761). On the other hand, the incident of the ruby being found in the belly of the fish would appear to be derived from Kalidas's *Shakuntala*.

Paan: A betel leaf preparation, chewed to sweeten the breath and as a digestive.

Pice: A coin of small denomination no longer in use.

HOW A TRIBAL BOY BECAME A KING

The *Bhuiyas* are an ancient tribe living in the forest highlands of central India. They worship various deities in Nature. But the Hindu influence is quite evident in this tale: the fairy is sent by Indra, the Hindu God of the Firmament; and there is reference to Yama, God of Death, and his kingdom, Yamaraj.

William Crooke, a British civil servant who was devoted to the study and collection of Indian folklore, recounted this tale in *The Indian Antiquary* of

March, 1894. He mentions that it was told to him by one of the most primitive members of the Bhuiya tribe, whom he met in the heart of the jungle.

THE HAPPY HERDSMAN

There are several variations on the theme of this folk-tale, which is still told in the villages of northern India. I first heard it as a boy, from an old Hindu lady who lived in the Mainpuri district.

In Hindu folklore, the banyan tree, with its spreading aerial roots, represents the matted hair of Shiva.

There are many folk-beliefs connected with snakes. They have the power of identifying and protecting the heirs of kingdoms. Ahichhatra, 'Snake Umbrella', a famous old town in the Bareilly district, has a legend of this kind which tells of a man who found Adiraja, the Ahir cowherd, who was destined to rule, sleeping in the shade of the outspread hood of a cobra.

Dhoti: A traditional garment, unsewn, worn by Hindu menfolk. It is passed round the waist, then between the legs, and fastened by being tucked in behind. It is shown being worn by male figures in Hindu and Buddhist sculptures of over two thousand years ago, and there has been no change in the garment since then.

THE TIGER-KING'S GIFT

This tale from South India is set in the time of the Pandya kings, who ruled in the far south five or six centuries before Christ. The dynasty had a long and prosperous career, extending into the Christian era. Embassies were sent to the Roman Emperor Augustus. We read (in Strabo's Roman Geography) of one embassy bringing curious presents, among them a man without arms, and a serpent ten cubits long! (This was probably a python).

Papanasam: Is the place of pilgrimage visited by Gangan and means 'expiation of sin'.

Pillaiyar: The elephant-headed God of Good Luck, is called Ganesh or Ganesa, in North India. He is also the God of Learning.

THE GHOST AND THE IDIOT

This folk-tale was first told to me by the mother of a young friend of mine, when I was a boy, spending a holiday with my friend in his village near Agra. His mother, who smoked a hookah in the evenings, was a great one for telling folk-tales – preferably ghost stories – before sending us to bed.

Peepul trees are held sacred, and are believed to be the abode of various spirits. A *Munjia* is the ghost of a Brahmin youth who has committed suicide on the eve of his marriage. There are many kinds of ghosts and tree-spirits in the villages in India.

BRAVE AND BEAUTIFUL

Rajputs: Literally sons of rajas or princes, the name by which several clans of India designate themselves. Almost all Hindus who have taken to soldiering claim a Rajput origin, a recognition of the superior martial qualities of the Rajput race.

Goddess Parvati: (at whose temple Sunderbai worships) is the wife of the God Shiva.

Ratan Singh: Singh (meaning Lion) is used as a sort of surname by the Rajput warrior class. Ratan is a first name.

SEVEN BRIDES FOR SEVEN PRINCES

This is a popular folk-tale in northern India, considerably influenced by Persian lore, in which fairies (Peris) abound. They were originally beautiful but malevolent sprites, often held responsible for comets, eclipses, failures of crops, etc. In later times they were seen as delicate, gentle fairy beings, helping the pure in heart to find their way to heaven.

A BATTLE OF WITS

My friend's mother, in her village near Agra, was fond of telling this story whenever I stayed with them. Needless to say she was a Jat lady. The tale is a popular one in the folklore of Northern India. The Banias are by tradition shopkeepers; the Jats are a farming community in Northern India.

"Chowdhri" (Chief) and "Shahji" (King) are forms of address used when two people are going out of their way to be very polite to each other.

The Jat's reference to God Indra withholding the seasonal rains is apt because Indra is the Lord of Thunder, whose lightning cleaves the clouds to bring forth rain. His attributes correspond to those of the Jupiter Pluvius of the Romans.

TORIA AND THE DAUGHTER OF THE SUN

This Santali legend was first rendered in English by Rev. F. T. Cole, Taljhari, Rajmahal, and appeared in the *Indian Antiquary*, Vol. IV, 1875.

The *Santals* are one of the aboriginal tribes of India, inhabiting the Santal Parganas, a district of West Bengal. They are noted for being industrious, truthful and kindly people. Good hunters, with spear, bow and arrow, they eat the flesh of most animals. They have four gods of the woods (Dryads), represented by four stones buried in a clump of trees called the Jairthan, and no Santal village can be settled till the Jairthan is established. They worship the Sun at the Jom Sin festival, when mysterious rites are performed in the forest. Their most solemn oath is taken when touching a tiger's skin.

THE WICKED GURU

This folk-tale comes from South India. M. N. Venkataswami includes it in his *Folklore from Dakshina-Desa* (1905).

Dwapara Yuga: In Hinduism, this was the third age of the world, extending to 864,000 years. In this age, goodness declined and mankind was assailed by calamities; few dared disobey their Gurus.

Sloka: A Sanskrit word, meaning a stanza or verse of four lines.

"AS YOUR LIBERALITY, SO YOUR VIRTUE"

This tale is illustrative of the Hindu concept of re-birth and Karma: your actions in this life will determine the nature of the next. I found it in G. H. Damant's 'Bengali Folklore: A Legend of Dinajpur' in the *Indian Antiquary*, Vol. I, 1872. G. H. Damant was a Deputy Commissioner of the Naga Hills, who fell a victim to the rebel Mozema Nagas during a rising of that tribe in October 1879.

Goddess Durga: Wife of the God Shiva, in her more terrible form. She has ten arms and in most of her hands are weapons. She is sometimes depicted as a beautiful yellow woman riding on a tiger, and is widely worshipped in Bengal.

Sheora trees: (*Trophis aspera*) are found in Bengal and Orissa. They have scabrous leaves which are used to polish horn and ivory. The bark is used medicinally, the leaves and sap for wounds. The berries are greedily eaten by birds.

THE SONG OF THE WHISTLING-THRUSH

Krishna: The most celebrated hero of Indian mythology, and the most popular of all the deities. Around him there has gathered a great mass of legend and fable.